THERAPEUTICS FOR AGGRESSION

THERAPEUTICS FOR AGGRESSION
Psychological/Physical Crisis
Intervention

Michael Thackrey, Ph.D.

Clinical Director
Sumner Mental Health Services
Gallatin, Tennessee

Adjunct Assistant Professor of Psychology
Vanderbilt University
Nashville, Tennessee

Sah-Dan
Tae Kwon Do Moo Duk Hae
Seoul, Korea

 **HUMAN SCIENCES PRESS, INC.**
72 FIFTH AVENUE
NEW YORK, N.Y. 10011-8004

Library of Congress Cataloging-in-Publication Data

Thackrey, Michael.
  Therapeutics for aggression.

  Bibliography: p.
  Includes index.
  1. Violence. 2. Crisis intervention (Psychiatry)
3. Restraint of patients. 4. Therapist and patient.
5. Medical personnel and patient. I. Title.
[DNLM: 1. Aggression. 2. Crisis Intervention.
Mental Health Services. WM 401 T363t]
  RC569.5.V55T48   1986   616.85′82   86-10557
  ISBN 0-89885-305-2

CONTENTS

5

ACKNOWLEDGMENTS

All photographs courtesy of William P. Henry, Ph.D.

Modeling courtesy of Stephen F. Butler, Ph.D., Greg Perfetto, Ph.D., William R. Roberts, Ph.D., Forrest Talley, Ph.D., and Noreen Thackrey.

All other figures courtesy of Rosalie Pearson.

Names, circumstances, and other identifiable information in case studies have been sufficiently altered to safeguard confidentiality.

PREFACE

This book is about the emergency assessment and management of patient aggression against mental health clinicians—aggression by patients against the very persons who attempt to help them. Such aggression is known to virtually every discipline, within almost every setting, and among nearly every clinical population. A special aspect of the mental health clinician's work with aggressive behavior is the overall purpose of *therapeutic* intervention, rather than mere self-protection: Clinicians need an approach to patient aggression which is consistent with the therapeutic mission.

Borrowing from the landmark work of others—and adding my own modest contributions—I have attempted to synthesize a comprehensive, integrated system of psychological and physical principles which allows the clinician to implement the highest quality crisis intervention while safely and humanely protecting the self and others. Expressly formulated for those mental health clinicians who deliver direct services (such as counselors, nurses, physicians, psychologists, social workers, and technicians, working in either inpatient or outpatient settings); or who educate, supervise, or consult to service providers; or who set policy and define standards, the *Therapeutics for Aggression* principles are also relevant to professionals working in alcohol/ drug, correctional, educational, medical/surgical, mental retardation, and residential settings.

I am honored—and humbled—to recall kind, generous acts of the many people who have helped me at crucial points in my life. I hope that in their hearts they know how I feel about them. Unique among them is the woman, Noreen, who makes my life whole and who has, through our children Timothy and Rebecca, made our lives one.

Michael Thackrey

Chapter 1

AGGRESSION AGAINST
THE CLINICIAN

Aggression against the mental health clinician has been a fact of professional life for many years. A German psychiatrist was fatally assaulted in 1849 (Stierlin, 1956; cited in Ekblom, 1970), and King Ludwig II of Bavaria murdered his own psychiatrist in 1886 (Lipp & Weingarten, 1975). By 1889, at least seven European psychiatrists had been killed by patients (Laehr, 1889; cited in Ekblom, 1970), and between 1901 and 1932 there was an average of one manslaughter per year in Italian mental hospitals (Bianchini, 1933; cited in Ekblom, 1970). Egaz Moniz, the Nobel prizewinner who performed the first prefrontal leukotomy, was shot and critically wounded by one of his patients in Portugal around 1940 (Walker, 1970). In the United States, the murders of psychiatrists and other mental health clinicians have been documented in recent years. A Boston area state hospital psychiatrist was killed while attempting to disarm a patient; and a New Haven, Connecticut psychiatrist was fatally shot by a patient whom he had seen only once but who had apparently incorporated him into a paranoid delusional system (Madden, Lion, & Penna, 1976). Turns and Gruenberg (1973) described the bludgeoning death of an attendant in a Poughkeepsie, New

York state psychiatric hospital, and Armstrong (1978) described the fatal shooting of a Washington, D.C. forensic psychiatric technician. Danto (1982–1983) described one Detroit area patient who killed a psychiatrist, and another who fatally stabbed a psychiatrist in a small Michigan city. In a 1980 Nebraska survey, Haffke and Reid (1983) found that during the previous year a psychiatric aide had been stabbed to death in an inpatient unit. Nelson (1983) reported four unrelated murders of psychiatrists by patients during a one-week period in 1981, and also described the shooting death of a Madison, Wisconsin senior psychiatric resident. Annis, McClaren and Baker (1984) described the fatal shooting of a psychiatrist by a patient whom he had seen only once, for ten minutes, the previous month. Scores of other such murders and major assaults have occurred.

Several surveys have attempted to estimate the percentage of mental health clinicians who have actually experienced some type of physical attack by a patient. Madden, Lion and Penna (1976) polled 115 Maryland psychiatrists working in a variety of settings and found that approximately 42% had been attacked at least once during their professional careers. Whitman, Armao and Dent (1976) surveyed a total of 184 Cincinnati psychiatrists, psychologists, and social workers in various settings: Of the 101 professionals responding, 74% had been attacked (24% within the previous year). Tardiff and Maurice (1977) sent questionnaires to all 210 psychiatrists working in central Vancouver: Of the 100 respondents, 40% indicated that their person, family, or property had been the object of patient violence. Ruben, Wolkon and Yamamoto (1980) interviewed 31 Los Angeles second- and third-year residents in psychiatry: Over 48% had been attacked during their two or three years of residency. Bernstein (1981) mailed an inquiry to 988 marriage and family counselors, psychiatrists, psychologists, and social workers in a variety of settings: Overall, more than 14% of the 453 respondents stated that they had been attacked, although for psychiatrists the rate was more than 42%. Hatti, Dubin and Weiss (1982) sent a questionnaire to 650 Philadelphia area psychiatrists working in various settings: Of 391 respondents, over 20% had been attacked. Most recently, Haffke and Reid (1983) surveyed all 88 psychiatrists in Nebraska: Of the 54 responding, more than 31% had been assaulted (over 16% during the preceding year).

Some studies have attempted to estimate the prevalence of aggressive behavior among patients within mental health facilities (in contrast to studies of aggression shortly before admission, e.g., Tardiff & Sweillam, 1980b). Quinsey and Varney (1977) closely monitored ward records, and interviewed patients and staff in an Ontario maximum security psychiatric unit for men: Their data show a rate of more than 0.9 assaults against staff per patient per year. Menzies, Webster & Butler (1981) mailed a questionnaire to 52 Canadian forensic psychiatrists: The 31 respondents estimated that 0.2% of their yearly total number of patients had actually assaulted them. Similarly, the professionals surveyed by Whitman, Armao and Dent (1976) estimated that 0.63% of their patients had attacked them. Lion, Snyder & Merrill (1981), using ward notes from a Maryland hospital with approximately 1500 patients, extrapolated a total of 1108 assaults against staff annually. Snyder (1983), working from ward logs in a Maryland state hospital with an approximate census of 1300, documented 1276 physical assaults against staff in one year and 1284 assaults the next year. Respondents to the Haffke and Reid (1983) questionnaire reported an average of approximately one incident per Community Mental Health Center per year in which a patient had threatened staff with a weapon, or attempted or completed a physical attack. Yesavage, Werner, Becker, Holman & Mills (1981) reviewed the clinical records of 26 male involuntary VA psychiatric patients in Palo Alto, California: Over 23% of these patients had behaved aggressively toward other patients or staff within one week of admission. A later study of records at the same hospital involving 110 male, mostly involuntary patients (Werner, Yesavage, Becker, Brunsting & Issacs, 1983) found that over 13% had behaved aggressively toward others within their first week on the unit. Ionno (1983) utilized a prospective design with special reporting procedures to study female long-term inpatients at a Connecticut nonprofit psychiatric unit with an average daily census of 23: An average of 11.2 assaults occurred against staff per month. In a methodologically rigorous investigation, Tardiff (1983a) utilized a structured rating instrument and trained surveyors at two large New York state psychiatric hospitals: Over 7% of both male and female patients were physically assaultive during a three-month period.

Aggressive behavior directed against the human services professional does not occur solely among adult mental patients; similar problems have been noted among adolescent (Elder, Edelstein & Narick, 1979) and child (Gair, 1980) mental health patients, correctional populations (Bidna, 1975), drug/alcohol clients (Piercy, 1984), elementary and secondary classes (Rossi, 1984), geriatric patients (Petrie, 1984), general medical/surgical hospital patients (Ochitill, 1983), hospital emergency room patients (Lion, Bach-Y-Rita & Ervin, 1969), the mentally retarded (Mehr & Hollerauer, 1984), outpatient private practice patients (Danto, 1975), private psychiatric hospital patients (Adler, Kreeger & Ziegler, 1983), residential treatment clients (Fixsen, Phillips, Dowd & Palma, 1981), social work clients (Schultz, 1984), university teaching hospital patients (Conn & Lion, 1983), and VA medical/surgical patients (Mikolajczak & Hagen, 1978).

Of course, the studies of patient aggression against the mental health clinician cited above are certainly not an exhaustive sample of the research, and one might take issue with particular methods, statistics and conclusions[1]. Some have even asserted that such aggression almost never happens in their particular setting; however, Whitman, Armao and Dent (1976) have concluded that assault is an "inevitable phenomenon that may occur at some time to every therapist" (p. 428). Even if one were to accept as accurate and representative the very lowest incidence estimate, because there are thousands upon thousands of mental patients even such a small percentage represents a very large absolute number of assaults.

Aggression against the clinician is pandemic and demands special attention and training. The remainder of this volume—while also relevant to other human service applications—will describe a system for preventing and managing patient aggression against the mental health clinician.

---

[1] A detailed analysis of research methodology is beyond the scope of this book; however, some limited comments will be made in a later chapter.

Chapter 2

OVERVIEW

Before discussing a system for preventing and managing aggressive behavior directed against the mental health clinician, we must first consider some important premises underlying the approach which will be presented.

NECESSITY OF PHYSICAL INTERVENTION

For two reasons, it is absolutely necessary to develop and disseminate appropriate principles and techniques of physical intervention as a means of coping with patient aggression: First, not every episode of potential or actual aggressive behavior can be resolved without physical intervention; and second, in those episodes in which nonphysical intervention might be possible, less than optimal clinician technique may fail to prevent (or may even precipitate) a physical attack.

While verbal intervention is of course to be preferred over physical intervention, some patients (e.g., the agitated psychotic, delirious, demented, or drug-intoxicated) may simply be so disordered that sustained, meaningful interaction is not possible. As Soloff (1983) has observed,

> The approach of "talking down" the potentially violent patient assumes that the patient can perceive the same causal reality as the clinician and, indeed, that verbal communication is meaningful at all. . . . These preconditions to communication may not be met. The occasional loss of life that has resulted from a physician's attempts to "talk down" violent patients serves as a stark reminder of our limited understanding of violence (p. 250).

Others (e.g., Jacobs, 1983; Taitz, 1984; Tardiff, 1984c) concur: Not every episode of potential or actual violence can be addressed nonphysically. Even among patients who might possibly be amenable to verbal intervention, when the patient is unknown to the clinician or when the clinician has for some other reason been unable to establish a therapeutic alliance, efforts at interpersonal management of the situation may prove unsuccessful. Furthermore, alternative control measures for violent episodes, such as voluntary medication or voluntary seclusion, may be contraindicated on medical or other clinical grounds (Gutheil & Tardiff, 1984; Soloff, in press). Of course, *most* situations can—with proper technique—be resolved without resort to physical intervention. However, such a resolution is highly dependent upon the skill of the individual, and skill varies widely from clinician to clinician. As Gair (1980) observes, "Some individuals have almost magically greater success setting nonphysical limits for extremely difficult patients than do most others. This, however, cannot be a basis for setting standards" (p. 16). No one is perfect in this regard and eventually every clinician is likely to miss the opportunity to avert a preventable episode (Conn & Lion, 1983; Quinsey, 1979; Quinsey & Varney, 1977) or inadvertently to precipitate an attack (which is, unfortunately, often the case [Madden, Lion & Penna, 1976; Ruben, Wolkon & Yamamoto, 1980]). Appropriate physical management contingencies must be available in the event of human error. Because of both patient factors and clinician factors, the need for physical intervention will never be completely eliminated from the professional mental health setting.

NECESSITY OF SPECIALIZED TRAINING

Training in the management of patient aggression has been likened to cardiopulmonary resuscitation (CPR) training (e.g., Nigrosh, 1983). It is preparation for an emergency situation that may occur infrequently; however, when that emergency actually happens there is no substitute for adequate preparation.

Unlike CPR, training in the management of patient aggression also serves an important primary preventive function: Training can make the clinician better able to avert violence. In one study ("Program . . . ," 1976), following staff training at a large Canadian psychiatric hospital, injuries directly related to patient activity declined 10.4% and employee hours lost due to patient assault decreased 31%. Although the overall frequency of assaults within a Canadian maximum security psychiatric facility remained unchanged, before training staff had been more likely than patients to be victims of assault; yet after training the staff became less likely than the patients to be assaulted (Quinsey, 1979). Infantino and Musingo (1985) found that state psychiatric hospital staff who had been trained were far less likely than untrained staff to be the victims of patient assault (3.2% versus 36.9%, respectively). Related measures, such as clinician education and training, implementation of explicit policies and procedures, and supervisory feedback, have been shown to lead to decreased utilization of seclusion, restraint, and medication (Davidson, Hemingway & Wysocki, 1984; Hay & Cromwell, 1980). Belanger and Mullen (1984) point out that staff social norms are among the primary determinants influencing choice of intervention technique, and that proper training can positively influence staff to utilize the less restrictive, more appropriate management procedures.

Some persons have expressed their opposition to the inclusion of physical management techniques in the context of training clinicians to prevent and manage patient aggression, claiming that such training may lead the clinician to overutilize such methods. However, this claim is contradicted by the research findings which imply that trained clinicians are involved in fewer physical altercations with patients than are untrained clinicians. Furthermore, high-quality training in management of the aggressive patient does not present physical management techniques in a vacuum, but rather considers them within the overall context of relevant legal, ethical, and clinical issues. Indeed, such training has been seen as a method for protecting the civil rights of patients and preventing patient abuse (cf. Nigrosh, 1983). The overall purpose of training in the prevention and management of patient aggression is *therapeutic*. The clinician must deliver high-quality clinical services to the patient, and in doing so must address the patient's inappropriate behaviors which impede treatment, yet which may represent the very essence of the condition for which treatment is indicated. Merely decreasing the likelihood of patient aggression is not an acceptable goal. Isolation and neglect of patients would certainly accomplish such a limited objective (Dietz & Rada, 1983a). Rather, the care and treatment of the patient—and the patient's eventual ability to provide internal controls—is at issue (Nigrosh, 1983). The technology employed must be consistent with the values traditionally associated with professional mental health services, and meet the same legal, ethical, medical, behavioral, and practical criteria as other mental health technologies.

The clinician's initial reaction to the threat of patient aggression is typically either to flee or to retaliate; if acted out, either represents a nontherapeutic response. The clinician may defend against these uncomfortable reactions with denial ("that patient is not actually dangerous"), reaction-formation ("this is a charming, interesting patient"), identification with the aggressor ("that patient had a right to hit me"), unrealistic helplessness and passivity ("if a patient really wants to hit you, there is nothing you can do about it"), omnipotent fantasy ("with sufficient care and skill, any patient can be 'talked down' "), overreaction ("the patient needed to be restrained after he started yelling at me"), suppression ("I don't want to think about what might happen"), repression ("I don't harbor any feelings at all about being hit"), projection ("that patient is actually afraid of me but doesn't realize it"), and the tendency to overutilize confrontation, seclusion, restraint, medication, referral, and discharge (cf. DiFabio, 1981; Hart, Broad & Trimborn, 1984; Lanza, 1983, 1984; Lion & Pasternak, 1973; Madden, 1977; 1982). These staff reactions also adversely affect the therapeutic milieu as a whole (Cornfield & Fielding, 1980; Felthous, 1984; Penna, 1983).

It is quite natural for the clinician to feel afraid of or angry toward a threatening person; however, the clinician's actions should be governed by therapeutic rather than by countertransferential issues. Yet how is the clinician to address these negative emotions, without being trained to do so? And is it unreasonable that the clinician should want to have a plan for action in the face of impending violence? How is the clinician to learn to cope with physically aggressive behavior, without training? Although many therapists have a thorough general clinical education, traditional training does not typically constitute adequate training for preventing and managing patient violence (Moran, 1984; Nigrosh, 1983). Di Bella (1979) has noted succinctly, "Staff will have to know how to restrain a patient, and they will not be able to unless someone trains them" (p. 335).

Specific training can significantly increase the clinician's ability to predict, prevent, and control aggressive patient behavior. This increase may be largely due to the development of confidence by the adequately trained clinician. In fact, Gair (1980) has remarked, "Training programs are effective to the degree to which they enhance staff confidence" (p. 16); gains in clinician confidence attributable to even a brief training program have been shown to endure for 18 months or more (Thackrey, in press). A realistic sense of ability to resolve emergent situations safely and effectively allows the clinician to convey stability and reassurance. The realistically confident clinician is able to access the full repertoire of trained professional techniques for assessment and intervention, decreasing the likelihood that a possible assault will actually take place.

It seems the best policy to base actions upon knowledge rather than upon ignorance. Inasmuch as physical intervention is a reality in the professional mental health setting, should we not implement it using the best available technology?

Lawful Biobehavioral Systems

A fundamental assumption of the approach to be presented is that human behavior is lawful. Although behavior is exquisitely complex, it does not "just happen" but rather functions according to orderly principles, and is potentially understandable as a self-regulating organismic system. The lawfulness of human behavior offers us the possibility of learning to predict and to control. Our understanding of biobehavioral principles is sketchy at present, and we may be unable to influence some of the mechanisms which we do understand. Because behavior is itself a complex phenomenon, the behavioral principles are also necessarily complex and not amenable to gross simplification. There are no simple techniques for behavioral assessment and intervention.

Crisis Intervention

Butcher and Maudal (1976) have defined the crisis situation as "one in which an outcome of some sort is inevitable, and prompt, correct action is consequently important" (p. 591); the word *crisis* actually derives from the Greek χρίσις meaning "decision" (Kittel, 1965). Such concepts seem especially useful in the present context. Violent emergencies can require immediate, decisive intervention; their outcome can be crucial for the future of all parties concerned. A true crisis can be seen as a potentially positive process. Although the capacity of the patient's (and the clinician's!) typical coping mechanisms may be outstripped in the crisis situation, as a consequence there may be an unparalleled opportunity to develop even more effective adaptive strategies in their stead (Caplan, 1964). While the crisis intervention approach is by no means identical with the brief or longer-term therapies, it is consistent with these and other sound clinical practices.

A corollary of the crisis intervention approach is an emphasis on prevention. Primary prevention averts a problem before it actually occurs, secondary prevention lessens the severity of an existing dysfunction, and tertiary prevention restores functioning following a disturbance (Caplan, 1964). An adequate system for managing aggressive behavior must focus upon early identification and intervention.

THE CENTRALITY OF JUDGMENT

A question often asked is, "What exactly should I do to manage an aggressive patient?" And, of course, there is no single, specific answer: An action which is effective in one situation may be disastrous in another. Although some clinicians seek hard-and-fast rules to determine their actions, few, if any, rules can be stated which are not endlessly contingent upon yet other rules. It is more realistic and productive to teach the clinician to analyze interventions in terms of underlying principles rather than to give a list of do's and dont's. Simply, *there is no substitute for judgment.* The material to be presented will, perforce, be expressed in terms of general principles. It is intended to help organize the clinician's independent thinking and to help develop the clinician's own effective techniques. The process of exercising judgment is a fundamental psychological mechanism which lies at the center of the conceptual, practical, clinical, and legal aspects of managing patient aggression.

PHILOSOPHICAL ISSUES

Certain philosophical issues must be discussed inasmuch as they relate to the clinician's conceptualization and approach to the violent patient. The system to be presented is based in part upon some explicit philosophical propositions.

First, the clinician must accept at least some degree of responsibility for whatever happens. Certainly the clinician is not entirely responsible for a patient's aggressive behavior; yet the clinician is part of an interrelated system within which the patient's aggressive behavior occurs. The effective clinician can always find some aspect of every incident which could have been handled better (e.g., not getting into the difficult situation in the first place, noticing a subtle yet telling premonitory sign, developing a superior intervention strategy). Such an orientation ensures that the clinician will not overlook possibilities for positive change, will continue to develop professionally, and will not become entrapped in feelings of powerlessness.

Second, the clinician must recognize that it is absolutely countertherapeutic to allow the patient to harm another person through inappropriate aggression. The clinician has not only a right but also a responsibility to protect the self and others. The patient who is allowed to harm another person suffers the effects of a distorted social learning experience which neither reflects nor prepares the patient for the "real world."

Third, the well-being of the aggressive patient is a central consideration; however, other patients and the clinician have equally important rights to safety. An individual clinician may elect to accept personal risk but must never be compelled to do so (merely being employed in a mental health setting does not constitute such an acceptance), and the clinician always has the right to self-preservation as the primary consideration.

The instance of attack is an inopportune moment to ponder basic assumptions and values. To be effective, the clinician must be comfortable with personal and professional philosophical issues.

Chapter 3

BIOBEHAVIORAL SYSTEMS
AND MECHANISMS

Behavior is an adaptive function of the organism. It consists in a dynamic system of interdependent mechanisms which enables the organism to survive. Behavior can be analyzed on (a) the physical level, and (b) the psychological level. While it may be somewhat artificial to separate these integrated levels, such a distinction proves conceptually useful in organizing our thinking about behavior.

THE PHYSICAL LEVEL

Physical properties determine behavioral possibilities. Anatomical and physiological (e.g., genetic, metabolic, hormonal, neurological, mechanical, and kinesic) phenomena directly control certain overt behaviors and certainly underlie others.

Some physical processes (e.g., respiration, digestion) serve rather directly to maintain and regulate vital internal functions; these processes demonstrate only a basic level of interaction with the external environment. Other physical processes (e.g., higher central nervous system activities) are necessary for more complex interactions with the environment; these processes serve as the matrix for psychological adaptation.

THE PSYCHOLOGICAL LEVEL

Both intrapsychic (e.g, affective, cognitive, volitional) and interpersonal (e.g., cultural, economic, political, social) processes can be conceptualized as essentially psychological mechanisms for response to and action upon the molar environment. Other people are often the most salient aspects of this molar environment. Such processes are based upon (and also affect) physical functions; psychological adaptation is necessary for the survival of the organism.

Meaningfulness

The central mechanism of psychological adaptation is the formation of an internal "picture" of the world. Percepts of the self, of other people, and of the rest of the environment are elements of this picture. The meaningfulness of this picture is essentially contextual: Meaningfulness is the relationship pattern of one person, object, or percept to another. The most basic level is interpersonal meaningfulness—that of the self in relationship to other people, and the ways in which one is similar and dissimilar to others. Behavior is purposive: People act according to the meaning of their percepts (for complete discussion, see Thackrey, 1982).

Feedback

Beliefs about the self and the rest of the world are either confirmed or disconfirmed by the effects of behavior. Feedback is both essential and inevitable.

The overall cycle of psychological adaptation is (a) perception of the self/environment, (b) meaningfulness of the percept, (c) purposive behavior, (d) feedback about the perceived effect of the behavior which affects (a), and so on, in an iterative process. This process is depicted in figure 1.

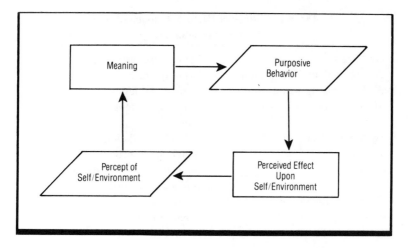

Figure 1.   An iterative process model of behavior.

AGGRESSIVE BEHAVIOR

Aggressive behavior is similar to other behaviors in that it can be analyzed on both physical and psychological levels.

Physical Aspects

The interaction between physical and psychological determinants of aggressive behavior is complex, and aggressive behavior in the clinical setting is seldom seen without some accompanying degree of psychopathology (cf. Bach-Y-Rita, Lion, Climent & Ervin, 1971; Barry, 1984; Dubin, 1981; Kutzer & Lion, 1984; Tardiff, 1984d). While sometimes a particular physical disorder (e.g., temporal lobe epilepsy) can be considered as the proximal cause of an aggressive episode, physical disorders more typically interact with psychological phenomena in producing aggression (e.g., alcohol intoxication and interpersonal provocation). Some physical conditions which can affect aggressive potential are listed in table 1.

Table 1.   Physical Factors Associated with Aggressive Behavior

akathisia	hyperthyroidism
alcohol or drug intoxication	hypoglycemia
alcohol or drug withdrawal	intracranial lesion
Alzheimer's disease	intracranial neoplasm
anemia	meningitis
cardiopulmonary insufficiency	mental retardation
delirium	metabolic disorder
dementia	normal pressure hydrocephalus
diabetes	nutritional disorder
electrolyte disturbance	pneumonia
encephalitis	renal disorder
endocrine disorder	seizure disorder
genetic disorder	septicemia
hepatic disorder	toxins
hormonal disorder	tricyclic antidepressant medication
hypertension/hypotension	vascular disorder

The clinician must remain alert to the possibility of a medical problem underlying any instance of aggressive behavior, especially in a patient whose cognitive or affective functioning has shown abrupt change, or whose clinical presentation includes confusion, disorientation, delirium, impaired concentration or memory, olfactory or visual hallucination, seizure, stereotypy, etc. (cf. Mark & Ervin, 1970; Rabin & Koomen, 1982). Jacobs (1983) advised that "the first rule of thumb is a high index of suspicion" (p. 259). Patients with physical etiology may prove responsive to techniques of psychological intervention in the course of crisis management, yet will of course need prompt medical attention as well.

Psychological Aspects

Like other behaviors, aggression is typically a contextual mechanism which furthers the survival of the organism. Aggression is not a phenomenon with primarily intrapsychic origins, but rather is a specific response to the perceived situation. Understanding aggressive behavior requires that one "see" the situation through the eyes of the patient.

Aggressive behavior almost always results from *fear* or from *anger*: Both affects are meaningful reactions (defensive and offensive, respectively) to perceived threats upon one's self or upon one's vital interests (Flannelly & Flannelly, 1982). Sometimes, of course, the perception of threat results from inaccurate or frankly psychotic ideas about the self and others; nonetheless, the emotional basis for aggression can be found in such thoughts and in the perceived meaning of the situation. While most clinicians may assume that aggressive behavior is an expression of anger, it is, instead, more likely that an aggressive act in the clinical setting arises out of fear (Nickens, 1984). A variety of psychological factors associated with increased likelihood of aggressive behavior are listed in table 2.

Aggression is usually infrequent because of the operation of *natural controls* over the elicitation and expression of aggressive behavior (cf. Lorenz, 1966). First, because aggressive behavior is purposive, it does not occur randomly but rather is only elicited within certain contexts. Second, aggressive behavior can also be inhibited. The expected negative consequences of aggressive behavior (retaliation, etc.) can inhibit aggression. Alternatively, the object of aggression can withdraw or make an "appeasement/submission gesture" which satisfies the aggressor and terminates the aggressive incident. Studies have illustrated some of these principles of aggression within the mental health setting. For example, Depp (1983) found that middle hierarchy inpatients most often aggressed against lower hierarchy patients, apparently in order to defend against what they perceived as threats to their social position. Levy and Hortocollis (1976) studied the incidence of violence on an inpatient unit with an all-female staff in contrast to another unit with both male and female staff members. Markedly fewer violent incidents occurred on the female-staffed unit (among other factors, female staff were believed to seem less threatening to patients and therefore were less provocative of aggression).

It is important to analyze aggressive incidents not only in terms of precipitants, but also in terms of the failure of natural controls on aggressive behavior. For example, one might find

Table 2. Psychological Factors Associated with Aggressive Behavior

affective lability	involuntary treatment
agitation	isolation
ambivalence toward clinician	jealousy
anger	limit-testing
anxiety	manic excitement
behavioral contagion	monetary dispute
blocked exit	obsessive compulsive disorder
catatonic excitement	overcontrol
childhood abuse	overdependency
cinema modeling	pain
clinician provocation	paranoia
confusion	personal space violation
crowding	personality disorder
cultural expectation	political grievance
delusion	post traumatic stress disorder
depression	psychosis
fear	ritualistic behavior
frustration	schizophrenia
grief	sexual difficulty
hallucination	social skills deficit
high ambient temperature	stress
homosexual panic	suicidal/self-mutilatory
humiliation	ideation/action
hyperkinesis	thought disorder
hypervigilance	undercontrol
impulse control disorder	vengefulness
interpersonal hierarchy disturbance	violent coping strategy
interpersonal loss	volition

that consequences for aggressive behavior had not been made apparent to a patient, or perhaps that a clinician could have assuaged a patient's anger by "backing down."

COMMUNICATION

The word "communication" derives from the Latin *communicā-re* ("to make common" [Oxford, 1933]). Meaning can be made common between individuals by signals of different kinds. Some of the specific signals are "universals," and others are common only to a given culture, class, etc. Communication signals are carried over verbal, paraverbal, kinesic, proxemic, and haptic channels (Harper, Wiens & Matarazzo, 1978; Heslin & Patterson, 1982).

Verbal

Verbal communications are spoken words; these actual words have both literal meanings and implied meanings. Verbal communications are usually the most salient of interpersonal behaviors, capable of conveying complex, abstract, and subtle meanings.

Paraverbal

Paraverbal communications are closely related to verbal communications, but they consist in the utterances and sounds which are not actual words (For example, a prolonged "umh" sound in a midsentence verbalization break might mean that the speaker is not yet finished talking, is thinking of what to say next, and is "reserving" the channel so that another person will not attempt to speak during that interval). Paraverbal signals also include silences, and the inflection, tone, and volume of speech.

Kinesic

Kinesic communications consist in meaningful bodily movements, such as body orientation and posture, eye contact and gaze, facial expression, gestures, and movement quality. Kinesic signals may be brief or long-term (e.g., a wink, or etched smile-lines in the face, respectively [Ekman & Friesen, 1975]).

Although not formally considered kinesic communications, a similar class of signals consists in natural physical appearance stimuli (e.g., physique, physiognomy) and "artifacts" (e.g., attire, cosmetics). These stimuli convey meaning (regardless of whether it is accurate or inaccurate, intentional or unintentional) from one person to another. Manipulating the attire variable, Rinn

(1976) found that incidents of aggressive behavior were more frequent during periods when inpatient psychiatric nursing personnel wore white uniforms rather than contemporary street clothing, apparently because of the meaning that the uniforms held for the patients.

Proxemic

Proxemic communications convey meaning through the use and structuring of space. Standing quite close to rather than far away from another person, looming above rather than remaining on the same level, or approaching directly rather than at an angle all convey distinct interpersonal messages.

Interpersonal distance can become quite crucial in volatile situations. As a patient becomes increasingly fearful or angry, the size of the "body-buffer zone" for comfortable interpersonal distance increases substantially (cf. Curran, Blatchley & Hanlon, 1978; Depp, 1976, 1983; Hildreth, Derogatis & McKusker, 1971; Kinzel, 1974, 1979; Roger & Schalekamp, 1976).

Related to interpersonal distance is the concept of territory. An invasion (whether deliberate or not) of another's territory can evoke fear, anger, and resulting aggression (Ardrey, 1966; Lorenz, 1966).

Haptic

Haptic communications occur through the sense of touch. While physical touching may or may not constitute part of a given clinician's interpersonal technique (handshake, hug, etc.), in some settings touch will occur routinely as an integral part of patient care and treatment (during administration of medication, examination, monitoring of vital signs, etc.). Who touches whom, the quality of the touch (e.g., comfortable or tense), and the reaction to the touch (e.g., avoided or welcomed) all are meaningful communications.

Integration

Under normal conditions, the different modalities of communication (verbal, paraverbal, kinesic, proxemic, haptic) are

harmonically integrated so that messages in one modality augment, substitute for, or even contradict messages in another
modality in a rich, meaningful pattern (Harper, Wiens &
Matarazzo, 1978). In the process of communication, while one
may attend to the verbal level, many other complementary aspects (especially kinesic and proxemic signalling) can function
without the fully conscious awareness of either party to the
communication, yet nonetheless have an important contextual
impact on the overall meaning of the communication.

Content

In violent crisis situations, the *process* of interpersonal communication can become exceedingly complex; however, the actual *content* of the communication between patient and clinician
tends to reflect certain common themes.

As previously discussed, the patient may experience *fear*
or *anger*; these feelings may be expressed, or acted out aggressively. From the patient's perspective, the clinician's behavior
is likely to seem either *friendly* or *threatening*, and either *firm*
or *yielding*. Most complex interactions can be conceptualized
along similar underlying dimensions (cf. Benjamin, 1982).

We communicate who we are. Because of the complexity
and subtlety of communication, it is not possible to convincingly
feign interest, concern, or compassion.

Chapter 4

A CONCEPTUAL SCHEMA FOR CRISIS ASSESSMENT AND INTERVENTION

CRISIS

The organism's biobehavioral mechanisms function so as to maintain homeostatic equilibrium. However, in a crisis situation, the capacity of the coping mechanisms may be pushed to—or beyond—their limits (cf. Caplan, 1964). Crises develop in four stages (displayed in figure 2): (a) the baseline level of functioning, in which an existing repertoire of behaviors addresses demands of everyday life; (b) the onset of a new, distressing situation and an attempt to adapt using the previously developed coping behaviors; (c) the failure of these existing coping behaviors to address the situation adequately, producing increased distress: Equilibrium is disturbed and functioning drops below the previous baseline; and (d) the decisive ("crisis") point: Either equilibrium becomes established around a lower (possibly deteriorating) baseline, or new coping behaviors and strategies are developed which successfully meet the demands of the new situation. In this latter case, functioning can return to previous baseline level or even beyond. Thus, the crisis situation is a potentially positive opportunity for the development

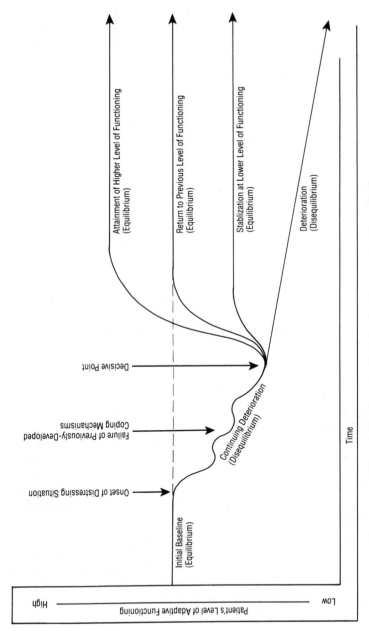

Figure 2.   Stages of crisis development and resolution.

of enhanced coping capacity and for the access of latent abilities. Only when observed out of context does a crisis appear as a discrete, precipitous, or unpredictable event. It is instead a rich sequence which allows ample opportunity for early identification, effective intervention, and beneficial resolution.

ACTUARIAL AND EMPIRICAL BASES FOR ASSESSMENT AND INTERVENTION

We simply do not have the facts necessary to formulate universal rules concerning crisis assessment and intervention. As McKenna (1983) has noted:

> Strangely, if a forensic psychiatrist were asked to testify in a case in which, let us say, one monkey attacked another, the testimony would be based on more complete information than a case involving a human. This is because a plethora of context-specific data on nonhuman primates are available. These data illuminate a wide range of social, ecological, and endocrinological circumstances under which these animals will be expected to act aggressively. Data on humans are much more complex, and sometimes they are absent altogether (p. 105).

This lack of factual information can be attributed to several factors. Comparatively little research has been performed. Direct clinical studies on violence in the professional setting are necessary (cf. Tardiff, 1983a; 1984c), but are difficult to carry out because clinicians are apt to be skeptical of their value, administrators are apt to fear embarrassment, and overall resources are few (Dietz & Rada, 1983a). We have not had a stratified sampling of professional disciplines, treatment settings, and clinical populations. Studies using questionnaires have typically been based upon small and distinctly nonrepresentative samples. Conclusions based upon review of institutional "incident reports" are also suspect: Lion, Snyder & Merrill (1981) compared such reports to daily ward notes and estimated that nearly five times as many assaults actually occurred than were formally reported. Sets of findings are not directly comparable with one another: Across different methodologies, there has been no consistent definition of aggressive behavior (cf. Dietz, 1981; Mulvey & Lidz, 1984) nor uniform denominator for calculating the incidence rate (cf. Tardiff, 1984c), and in some cases patient-to-patient assault has been reported confluently with patient-to-clinician assault. The few data we do have are unenlightening. Some validated characteristics of violent patients may occur with high frequency among nonviolent patients as well, and thereby fail to predict who will *not* become violent (Tardiff, 1984c); some variables correlated with an increased risk of violence (e.g., youth, psychosis) may be so common as to be virtually useless for differential prediction (Dietz & Rada, 1983a). Statements relating violence to diagnostic category are of limited validity due to the notorious unreliability of nosological labels, and it is debatable whether some characteristics associated with increased risk of violence (e.g., personality disorder, drug- or alcohol-abuse) even constitute true mental illness (Rabkin, 1979). Many variables overlap one another considerably (e.g., age and diagnosis) and therefore do not provide additive, orthogonal information (Tardiff & Sweillam, 1979). Even if we had highly sensitive and specific predictors, in situations where aggressive behavior is a low-frequency event, formal efforts at prediction would be highly biased because of the "base-rate problem" (cf. Megargee, 1976, 1981; Reinhardt, 1979); in fact, in such situations it might even be more accurate on the whole to predict that *no one* will become violent, rather than to prognosticate differentially even on the basis of valid predictor variables (Steadman, 1983). Perhaps most important, aggressive behavior has not typically been conceptualized in the sophisticated manner necessary to account for the complex interaction of variables such as biophysiology, environment, situation, precipitants, social dynamics, and patient/clinician motivations, stressors, and related personality variables (cf. Depp, 1983; Megargee, 1976, 1981; Monahan, 1982, 1984; Mulvey & Lidz, 1984; Quinsey, 1979; Steadman, 1983; Tardiff, 1984c).

It is obvious that the present state of empirical knowledge is far too limited to serve as an adequate basis for predicting and managing aggressive behavior. However, if assessment and intervention on the basis of empirically validated criteria are not possible, what is the alternative?

JUDGMENT AS THE BASIS FOR ASSESSMENT AND INTERVENTION

We may have access to an array of assessment data, and we may be capable of implementing a vast armamentarium of intervention techniques, but the central mechanism that subsumes the intersection of assessment and intervention is *judgment*; in a crisis situation there is no other basis for decision making. Judgment is an internal process of integrating information from a variety of sources.

Sources of Information

One of the two most useful sources of information is the *patient's present behavior*. As previously discussed, this behavior can be analyzed on physical and psychological levels; communications consist in verbal, paraverbal, kinesic, proxemic, and haptic signals. Such data are meaningful only *in context* for that given individual and the present situation. The key to understanding any sample of behavior is to know the *meaning* that the behavior holds for that person. Nonimmediate, nonobservable data may provide the clinician with background information which will affect the clinician's understanding of the present situation. Examples of such data are the client's previous behavior in similar situations (and the ways in which it may be similar to and different from present behavior: especially worth noting is any *change* from the patient's previously characteristic behavior), the clinician's knowledge of empirical correlates of aggressive behavior (e.g., age, sex, diagnosis), etc. However, such data may be nonexistent or unavailable to the clinician. In any event, the client's immediate behavior is one of the most important sources of data upon which to make assessment and intervention judgments. The second major source of data is the *clinician's immediate affective reactions* to the patient's behavior and the situation ("gut feelings," "hunches," "vibes," and the like). Conceptually, such feelings can represent one of two phenomena: (a) the clinician is actually sensitive to and reacting to some nonverbal aspect of the patient's behavior (perhaps so subtle or rapid that it will have an effect without being fully attended to by patient or clinician), or (b) the clinician is reacting to some other internal stimulus which is not directly related to the patient (e.g., displaced or otherwise unintegrated clinician affect). Of course, the major clinical skill is to differentiate patient-induced from self-induced feelings. The clinician must be able to evaluate accurately not only the patient, but also the self. Rather than defending against patient-induced fear or anger, the clinician should attempt to become sensitive to such feelings and to utilize them as a therapeutic tool (cf. Beier, 1966; Nadelson, 1977; Nickens, 1984).

The most essential data, therefore, are (a) the patient's present behavior, and (b) the clinician's affective reactions. The process of *judgment* integrates these kinds of information and is the basis for "making sense of the situation" (assessment) and "deciding what to do" (intervention). The use of judgment in this manner is merely the conscious utilization of the normal mechanisms of human interpersonal information processing as a clinical procedure. Every reasonably healthy clinician is presumed to have the ability to function in this manner.

Although methodological shortcomings seriously limit the validity of its conclusions, research consistently highlighting the inaccuracy and limitations of clinical judgment is nonetheless sobering (cf. Quinsey, 1979; Werner, Rose, Yesavage & Seeman, 1984; Wiggins, 1973). The clinician must remain cognizant of the fallibility of judgment, and the insidious nature of judgmental error. No one is easier to fool than oneself. However, judgment remains the sole mechanism whereby the clinician can rapidly synthesize qualitatively different data (including indicators which are refractory to objective measurement) and plan an appropriate intervention—decided advantages in the immediacy of the crisis situation.

The Clinical Process of Crisis Assessment and Intervention

The essential clinical process of crisis assessment and intervention is to (a) make contact with the situation and gather information from all appropriate sources; (b) use judgment to integrate the information and to arrive at some hypothesis about what is going on and what might work; (c) take action according to the hypothesis, (d) get feedback (additional information) from the situation and the effects of the action taken, and return to (a); this process is iterated until the crisis is resolved. This conceptualization of assessment and intervention is depicted in figure 3.

Considered in this manner, assessment and intervention are not distinct but rather are interactive facets of the selfsame process. A crisis situation often demands immediate intervention, and the way that the patient responds to the intervention is itself assessment data.

Because both crises and interventions are *processes*, the clinician must recognize that the essential task is to *work with* the crisis rather than to short-circuit it. The crisis is not to be feared but to be recognized for what it is—an interplay of adaptive behavioral mechanisms, with significant potential for the devel-

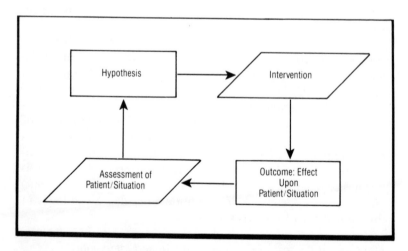

Figure 3.   The clinical process of crisis assessment and intervention.

opment of enhanced functioning. Likewise, the clinician's own internal confusion must not be resisted nor reacted to with increased distress, but rather understood as a sign of intimate engagement with the patient and the situation, and a potential source of information and guidance. The stock advice to "remain calm" is probably not only impossible but is possibly countertherapeutic as well. The clinician must have strength and compassion in order to be a vehicle for the transformation of chaos into order.

Chapter 5

PSYCHOLOGICAL INTERVENTION TECHNIQUES

Proper clinical technique consists in applying knowledge of behavioral systems and mechanisms to the immediate situation. Depending upon the situation, any given procedure may be either indicated or contraindicated. For example, allowing a patient to shriek and rail may in one case be therapeutic (if it occurs in a cathartic/ventilatory process in place of physical acting-out) or countertherapeutic (if it occurs in the course of spiraling loss of control leading to physical acting-out). The central component of proper clinical technique is *judgment*. Within the perspective that all clinical technique is ultimately contextual and a function of judgment, it is possible to specify some principles for choosing a particular course of crisis assessment/intervention.

The Therapeutic Relationship

First, the clinician must pay particular attention to the quality of the therapeutic relationship with the patient. This relationship will begin with the very first moment of contact. At the very least, the clinician must treat the patient with respect. Empathy is a desirable attribute of the relationship; yet one cannot always empathize with a hostile, threatening patient (cf. Ellman, 1984). It is not possible to simulate empathy; similarly, clinician confidence cannot be faked convincingly. Such attempts are only likely to render the clinician ineffective. Rather than attempting to "turn off" patient-induced feelings such as fear or anger, the clinician should instead attempt to become even more sensitive to these affects and to utilize them as a measure of the therapeutic process. It is sometimes appropriate to share feelings of personal discomfort with the patient (depending, of course, upon the particulars of the situation and the patient's capacity to respond favorably to the communication), and to explore the patient's discomfort-producing interpersonal behaviors (cf. Strupp & Binder, 1984). Negative feelings must eventually be addressed; any misunderstanding between clinician and patient must not go unresolved indefinitely. In the event of intractable, nontherapeutic transference/countertransference, consideration should be given to providing the patient with a different clinician; when this difficulty is believed to be primarily a function of patient discomfort in forming a relationship with *any* other person, all parties concerned might be more at ease in allowing the patient to seek sessions from a pool of different clinicians on a "P.R.N." basis (cf. Lion, Madden & Christopher, 1976; Madden, 1982; Richmond & Ruparel, 1980; Thackrey, 1985) and so to dilute transference/countertransference phenomena. A positive relationship between clinician and patient certainly decreases the likelihood of violence against that clinician and in time of crisis the clinician may appeal to this relationship or directly request appropriate behavior of the patient.

Behavioral Alternatives

Second, the patient must be allowed an acceptable alternative to any inappropriate behavior which is blocked by the clinician. A situation must not be structured so that the patient can meet needs only in dysfunctional ways. Even a docile person will fight when no alternative is perceived. Although it is of course preferable to elicit proposed behavioral alternatives from the patient, at times it will be incumbent upon the clinician to provide alternatives for the patient. Options may be limited by both patient and situational variables, so the clinician's creativity and judgment are paramount. While elicitation of new coping strategies from the patient represents an excellent outcome to the crisis situation, at times the lesser goal of resolving a situation short of violence is more appropriate even though the patient may not be presented with the opportunity to develop enhanced coping ability during the process. To this end, the clinician may take direct palliative action "in reality" (e.g., removing the source of patient distress, meeting the needs of the patient). Verbalization is to be encouraged over acting-out: The patient must be given plenty of "air time," and attentive silence is often the clinician's best technique. The clinician must be prepared to ask the patient directly about aggressive or homicidal ideations (Ellman, 1984; Lion, 1978; Madden, 1982) in much the same way that suicidal ideations are routinely probed.

Working with the Crisis

Third, the clinician must work *with* the crisis process rather than against it, understanding the patient's behavior as an adaptation effort. Short-circuiting the process with a temporary solution may at times be necessary, yet at other times be less than optimally effective in the long run. Although there are no universal pathognomonic signs of violence, unprecipitated assault is quite rare if indeed it exists at all: Instead, there occurs typically (a) a prodrome, (b) an identified "incident," and (c) a reintegration. The clinician can optimize crisis outcome through early identification and intervention. The patient can then be assisted in working through the various phases of the process. The clinician must be wary of the situation that is too easily resolved. Crisis theory suggests that an adequate reintegration had not taken place; with troublesome underlying issues inadequately addressed a further flare-up might be likely.

The Patient's Perception

Fourth, the clinician must attempt to understand the patient's perception of the situation. At times a reasonable request may be imbedded within a seemingly outrageous patient demand, and by the same token the patient may inaccurately perceive the clinician's position on an important matter. Many clinical impasses have their roots in such inaccuracies of person-perception. For the clinician working with a patient who is capable of processing verbal feedback, the following impasse negotiation/percept validation algorithm (illustrated in figure 4) is suggested as a clinical vehicle:

1. The patient states the patient's own view of the situation or problem.
2. The clinician then states the clinician's understanding of what the patient has just said.
3. The patient corrects inaccuracies in the clinician's recounting of the patient's view.
4. The clinician then restates the patient's view. If the patient indicates that it is still inaccurate, steps 3 and 4 are reiterated until the patient indicates that the clinician is verbalizing an accurate account of the patient's view.
5. The clinician then states the clinician's own position on the matter.
6. The patient states the clinician's position.
7. The clinician corrects any inaccuracies in the patient's recounting of the clinician's position.
8. The patient restates the clinician's view. If it is inaccurate, steps 7 and 8 are reiterated.

The "processing" of perceptions in this manner allows the clinician to validate both clinician and patient experience, and gives the clinician numerous opportunities for intervention and subtle restructuring of the patient's perceptions through affect-identification (sensitization to feelings), catharis/ventilation (discharge of affect), distraction/redirection (guiding attention onto more appropriate activity), education (providing relevant infor-

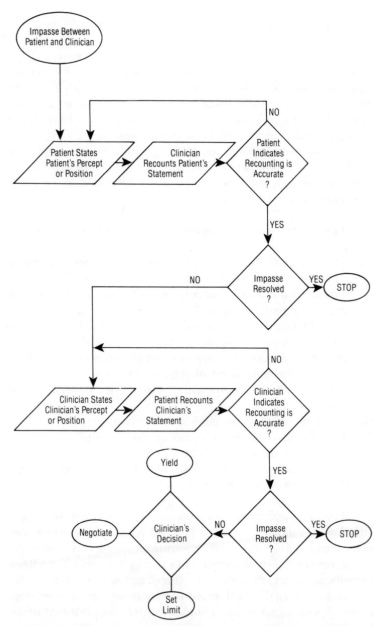

Figure 4.   The impasse negotiation/percept validation algorithm.

mation), focusing (maintaining attention on potentially useful material), interpretation (meaningful explanation), labeling (verbal designation), reframing (reconceptualization of facts within new context), and summarization (brief recapitulization). The clinician's skillful use of both open-ended and closed questions can subtly bring the patient into contact with important material.

Should the process become "stuck" at some point, the clinician should attempt to find at least some area of agreement and work from there, being willing to accept a temporary solution provided that there will be a later opportunity after the crisis to work out a more permanent solution. One of the best techniques for helping the patient in this manner consists in breaking complex problems into smaller, assimilable components. If the patient has excessive difficulty in negotiating a particular matter, the clinician may attempt to restructure it into manageable proportions. Certainly one is well advised to deal with one issue at a time, and with one person at a time.

Hierarchical Organization of Communication Channels

The various communication channels (verbal, paraverbal, kinesic, proxemic, and haptic) can be conceptualized in a hierarchical order: This hierarchical order is depicted in figure 5. Channels relatively lower in this hierarchy convey information which is less complex, less abstract, and typically less "conscious" than information conveyed via the relatively higher channels. Whether due to overwhelming emotional distress, functional or organic impairment, or other factor, as the patient becomes increasingly impaired *communication functions are lost from the 'top down'*. That is, communication on the verbal level is typically the first to be adversely affected (e.g., the patient may argue unreasonably, or even appear to be thought-disordered) yet communication may still be effective on other levels (the patient may still respond favorably to a soothing tone of voice and nonprovocative posture). A patient who is severely disordered may not be amenable to verbal, paraverbal, or even kinesic communications; however, such a patient might respond favorably to the proxemic communication of allowing ample

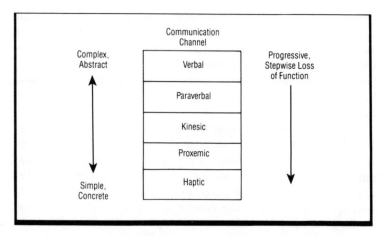

Figure 5. Hierarchical conceptualization of communication channels.

interpersonal distance or offering isolation. Finally, even violently agitated patients have shown sufficiently positive response to soothing, reassuring haptic (and other) communication signals (from a sincere, capable, highly experienced practitioner) to allow the safe removal of restraining devices. It is important to note that the *primary* communication may have passed from the verbal to a nonverbal channel in an upset yet coherent patient. Even though the clinician might be able to talk meaningfully with that patient, whether the patient's distress actually becomes acted out physically against the clinician may not be a function of what the clinician says but rather be immediately related to the clinician's tone of voice, posture, interpersonal distancing, etc. A major clinical task is to find the channel within which the most important meaning can be made common with the patient.

The clinician will typically want to convey a message that is congruent across the different channels: For example, in *confronting* a patient, the clinician might stand *facing* the patient while using other firm "body language" (kinesics and proxemics), a strong tone of voice (paraverbalization), and direct language (verbalization). Perhaps a practitioner specifically skilled in deliberate, paradoxical contradiction between (or within) communication channels (e.g., Haley, 1973; Noone, Molnar & Hopper-Small, 1979) might want to consciously give conflicting verbal and nonverbal messages. However, most clinicians are well advised to beware of inadvertently confusing the patient in this manner.

Channel-Specific Considerations

Verbal.   In time of crisis, the clinician should speak clearly and concretely. Abstract or vague language may be confusing to the patient, and the clinician must choose words very carefully.

Paraverbal.   The clinician should speak without undue speed or pressure of speech; tone of voice is often all-important. Sometimes whispering to a shouting patient (or asking the patient to repeat what the patient has just said) can get the patient to modulate voice volume.

Kinesic.   The clinician should model appropriate behavior, refraining from sudden movements. The clinician's eye contact convincingly conveys what words sometimes cannot: A fixed gaze into the patient's eyes may be perceived as hostility, whereas breaking eye contact can be seen as friendliness or appeasement. Likewise, the clinician's facial expression communicates quite directly to the patient. Posture is also a powerful signal. A sideways or 45-degree body angle toward the patient (as opposed to confronting) is usually considered the least threatening to the patient.

Proxemic.   Typically, the clinician should afford the patient plenty of interpersonal space unless the clinician has a specific reason for doing otherwise. A patient who is extremely distressed may feel crowded even when afforded a very large body-buffer zone. Often it is advisable to work with such patients in a very large room or out-of-doors (cf. Edelman, 1978), and walking (or other physical exercise) during a crisis may become an opportunity for the patient to "motor off" tension. Access to an exit can also become a high priority for both patient and clinician (cf. Ellman, 1984; Jacobs, 1983; Nickens, 1984). If at all possible, both parties should have access to their separate egress so that in a state of panic the patient will not perceive the clinician as an obstacle to flight, nor will the clinician become unduly frightened or trapped by an angry patient. When only one exit is available, it may be possible to arrange seating so that both parties have equal access. In situations where even that measure is not possible, as a last resort the clinician should sit next to the door and be alert for the necessity of rapidly moving out of the patient's way. In such a situation it may be advisable to leave the door open during the session; alternatively, the patient may feel less "trapped" if offered beverage or food, the use of telephone or restroom, etc. The patient's family and friends should be assessed in terms of whether they may be an asset (or a liability) in managing patient apprehension: If appropriate, the session may be conducted with a relative or friend of the patient present. The clinician should always be especially cautious when dealing with an unknown patient, and take a moment to assess briefly (e.g., greet patient in waiting room rather than have someone bring the patient into the office; engage in "brief socialization" outside) before entering an office with the patient. Secretarial and other staff should be trained to spot and notify the clinician of patients who appear to be upset or agitated (Nickens, 1984); the clinician should avoid working in isolation, and should arrange for another person to check periodically when working with a risky patient by means of telephone calls that can be answered yes or no (cf. Edelman, 1978); in some institutions the code word "Dr. Armstrong" is used to request assistance unobtrusively (Dubin, 1981).

Of course, the clinician should avoid approaching a volatile patient from behind; in general, an arcing 45-degree angle of approach is the least threatening; staying physically lower than the patient is usually nonthreatening and can even be seen as appeasing. The clinician must also be cognizant of the patient's perception of property and territory. For example, patients sometimes "own" particular corners of a psychiatric unit dayroom, or consider certain chairs "theirs." Certainly the clinician's office is seen as foreign turf. In order to decrease the patient's perception of threat it is sometimes beneficial to meet in "neutral" territory (such as a cafeteria or park).

Haptic.   Haptic techniques must be utilized judiciously. A handshake, touch, or hug can be a powerful therapeutic tool only (a) if the clinician is comfortable doing it, and (b) the clinician is absolutely certain that the patient is willing to be touched. A gesture intended by the clinician to convey warmth and caring may be misinterpreted by a distressed patient as a threatening invasion, so caution is essential; however, properly implemented, such techniques can be uniquely effective.

THE ASSESSMENT/INTERVENTION MATRIX

The aggressive patient typically experiences either *fear* or *anger*; the clinician's actions can be conceptualized as either *yielding* or *firm*. These possibilities form the matrix shown in table 3. The essential assessment task is to differentiate the fearful patient from the angry patient; the essential intervention task is to determine whether a yielding or a firm approach is indicated. Of course, sound clinical judgment lies at the heart of both tasks. In absence of other information regarding a specific patient and context, the clinician may be guided by the following two points: First, as previously discussed, aggressive patient behavior is more commonly due to fear than to anger. Second, a yielding rather than firm approach may be preferable initially; as the situation develops, it is generally easier to change from yielding to firm than vice versa.

The four cells of this matrix are a means for the clinician to conceptualize prototypical approaches to the patient; these approaches are implemented through the various (verbal and nonverbal) communication channels:

1. In response to the fearful patient, the clinician may judge that *threat-reduction* is the first priority. In some cases, threat can be reduced by words (e.g., "It's safe here now"), by confident and reassuring tone of voice, gesture, posture, etc. In other

Table 3.   Assessment/Intervention Matrix

		Clinician's Response	
		Yielding	Firm
Patient's Experience	Fear	Threat-reduction	Alliance
	Anger	Appeasement	Limit-setting

cases, when the clinician is perceived as threatening, the only effective means of reducing threat may be for the clinician to offer the patient isolation or the opportunity to leave (or for the clinician to leave!), permitting the patient to eventually seek contact on the patient's own terms. To attempt to establish contact prematurely with the patient may only precipitate a defensive attack.

2. In response to the fearful patient, the clinician may alternatively judge that an *alliance* with the patient is possible, so that although the perceived threat is not directly diminished the patient's perceived capacity to cope with the threat is bolstered. In such a case the patient may respond favorably to firm supportive measures such as the clinician's offer to stay with the patient and to be a situational ally (cf. Havens, 1980; Lorenz, 1966) in which common enemies are "shared." Occasionally a fearful patient will request (and typically should be allowed) medication or even mechanical restraint as a means of enhancing coping ability. Just as some fearful patients will react negatively to any direct supportive attempt by the clinician, others will instead respond positively to firm, strong support.

3. In response to the angry patient, the clinician may judge that yielding to the patient in an *appeasement* process is the intervention of choice. An example of appeasement is the apology from the clinician to the patient for some actual error or slight. This apology can have a positive effect upon both parties and can be a positive social learning experience for the patient. At other times appeasement might not be considered justified in terms of the interpersonal process (in that the patient uses the

threat of aggression as a means to meet needs) yet might be the only means available to the clinician to preclude overt violence. In such a case it is arguable that the dilatory effects of this learning are less than those of an actual real-time practice of assaultive behavior. Certainly such occurrences will need adequate review and remediation after the immediate crisis has been resolved. In addition to verbal communications, appeasement can be conveyed by tone of voice, by appearing "small," by staying lower than the patient with head down, etc. Unlike yielding to the fearful patient (intended to reduce threat), yielding to the angry patient is intended to allow the patient to discharge affect short of physical blows.

4. In response to the angry patient, the clinician may alternatively judge that firm *limit-setting* is in order. Although the ultimate goal is for the patient to develop internal controls. (cf. Nigrosh, 1983) it is often necessary for the clinician to set external limits on the behavior of the patient who has not yet developed such internal controls. Limit-setting can be a positive therapeutic technique as it allows the patient to understand which behaviors are prescribed and which are proscribed; it gives the patient realistic expectations regarding the behavior of clinicians and others, thus allowing the patient to get approval rather than disapproval; it may keep the patient from doing something that will prove humiliating to the self or harmful to others; and it can convey clinician concern and competence (Lyon, 1970). Patients typically want and expect the clinician to be competent, fair, and in control of the situation. In the final analysis, limit-setting with the patient's best interests at heart is likely to be eventually understood and appreciated by the patient. At an appropriate time after a limit-setting intervention, the meaning of the limit-setting within the context of the therapeutic relationship must be addressed. The clinician should be cognizant of the fact that some degree of resistance to limit-setting can be a positive, adaptive phenomenon. Generalized, docile acceptance of imposed limits is dysfunctional.

LIMIT-SETTING TECHNOLOGY

There are two major methods of limit-setting ("direct" and "indirect"), and principles which are common to both methods.

The direct method of limit-setting involves giving the patient direct commands. The indirect method involves giving the patient a series of choices among acceptable behavioral alternatives. The clinician must judge whether the direct or the indirect method is the procedure of choice depending upon the relative anticipated consequences for the patient's subsequent behavior. Some patients will be angered by and vigorously resist directives; other patients will be confused or frightened by choices.

Common Principles

The clinician must recognize that any external control over another's behavior is necessarily temporary; only with great effort can one monitor and enforce behavioral limits. Any blocked intention must be allowed an acceptable alternative, and the clinician should require only that degree of behavioral change which is absolutely necessary. Reality-based, natural consequences of behavior are a more useful focus than are consequences created by the clinician. Consistency is absolutely essential.

Whenever possible, the clinician should attempt to allow the patient to make behavioral choices (cf. Lyon, 1970; Sheard, 1985). Limit-setting technology which emphasizes the centrality of choice has positive philosophical, legal, ethical, pragmatic, and therapeutic merits. The clinician who has a basic reservation with such an approach should explore thoroughly what is likely to be a personal rather than a professional issue.

Commands and alternatives regarding both expected and prohibited behaviors must be stated *concretely* and in terms of actions which can be performed *immediately*. Whenever possible, directives and alternatives should be expressed in positive terms ("do this," which describes acceptable behavior) rather than negative terms ("don't do that," which conveys no acceptable alternatives). The best limits are absolute rather than relative (such as, "don't bang on the window," rather than "don't bang on the window so hard"). Specific time frames regarding compliance, choice of alternatives, and consequences must also be given.

The clinician must know the actual enforceable limit and consequences of its violation. Consequences of violating the limit must be made explicit and specific, and the clinician must not describe either a positive or a negative consequence which the clinician is unable or unwilling to deliver. With proper clinical technique, neither bribes nor threats will be necessary.

An essential aspect of limit-setting is for the clinician to determine whether negotiation is even a possibility. Generally, the greater the degree of cognitive impairment (including temporary compromise due to emotional distress) the less able is the patient to process negotiation appropriately. In such a case the clinician must be prepared to take direct action. Limit-setting may need to be implemented early rather than late in the course of clinical events to prevent further deterioration of the patient and the situation. On the whole, limit-setting is typically utilized too late rather than too early by well-meaning but inexperienced clinicians.

Once the need for a behavioral limit has been established, the clinician may explain the limit and its rationale but must avoid engaging in argument rather than negotiation. During limit-setting, deferral of clinician consequential action is appropriate so long as the patient is actively processing the clinician's command or choices offered; however, this period should be relatively brief, with superfluous discussion avoided when attempts at negotiation have been exhausted (cf. Soloff, in press).

Direct Technique

The essential procedure for the direct technique of limit-setting is to *state clearly and specifically the required or prohibited behavior*. Although the clinician may additionally describe consequences of violating the limit, such a statement is not an essential aspect of this direct method of limit-setting. With a confused or emotionally overwhelmed person, describing the consequence may only produce further dysfunction; in such a case, only the directive (in its positive or negative format) should be given. Refocusing and reorientation of the confused patient may be necessary, along with repetition of the directive. The limit should always be presented as a factual statement about required behavior (and consequences). State the limit as a concrete directive, never as a request, as advice, as bribery, as punishment, or as a challenge.

Indirect Technique

The essential procedure for the indirect technique of limit-setting is to *divide the will to resist by causing the patient to choose among acceptable behavioral alternatives*. It is easy for the patient to oppose a single directive; however, because attention cannot be focused simultaneously upon two or more alternatives, resistance to any particular one is diminished. The clinician subtly maintains control by limiting the choices while giving the patient responsibility for choosing. If necessary, the clinician acknowledges the patient's wishes and dissatisfaction with the clinician for setting a limit. The clinician first states the concrete alternatives, and then gives the patient the opportunity to choose. Should the patient refuse to make any choice, the clinician can make a time-bound conditional choice on behalf of the patient (such as, "if you do not choose to walk to your room in five seconds, I will take that to mean that you choose for us to carry you to your room"). Even when the situation results in the clinician making the final choice in this way, any resistance shown is typically far less than had the patient not been given a choice.

ILLUSTRATIVE CASES

Case number 1.   L. was a 23-year-old white male, an athletic weight lifter who had been very popular in high school. L. had been playing football in the street with some friends; he ran out for a pass and kept on running for several miles toward the end of town, where he hailed a cab and had the driver take him 45 miles north to the next city. During the ride the cab driver noticed that L. was behaving and speaking oddly; when L. was unable to pay the fare at the conclusion of the ride the driver called the police who transported L. to the inpatient unit of the local Community Mental Health Center. L.'s behavior deterio-

rated; he became quite agitated and threatening, and re-
fused medication although he went voluntarily to the seclusion room. In locked seclusion, L. screamed for hours;
he clawed a large hole in the wall and could reach his arm
into the next room; were it not for the steel studs he might
have succeeded in making one large room out of two
smaller ones. Although the attending psychiatrist gave an
order for mechanical restraints and medication, L. threw
several male technicians back through the doorway when
they attempted to enter, seriously injuring one. L. recoiled
from the hole he had made in the wall, and writhed in ag-
ony as he apparently hallucinated rats coming in from the
next room. A highly educated, highly experienced female
nurse, middle-aged and perceived by staff and patients
alike as a "strong earth mother" addressed the fear component of L.'s behavior, first by spending several hours just
outside the open seclusion room door without entering.
She spoke softly and directly to L., and eventually entered
the seclusion room where she stayed against the wall beside
(rather than in front of) the door, giving L. as much interpersonal distance as possible. After more than two hours,
L. accepted her offer of milk in a paper cup and eventually let her hold him by the hand. L. later took oral medication administered by the nurse, who stayed with L. for
three full days, sleeping outside of the seclusion room on
the floor until L.'s condition had improved sufficiently for
him to leave the seclusion room and participate in the
therapeutic milieu.

Case number 2.   H. was a 28-year-old white female, a
former nun and high school teacher. Her behavior had become problematic over the course of several years, with
bouts of agitated depression and suicidal gestures. Although she sought help from a crisis center, she always
managed to foil the clinicians' efforts to help her, eventually alienating virtually every mental health professional
with whom she came into contact. For example, she once
lay down in front of a clinician's car so that the clinician
could not go home at the end of the shift, and twice threat-

ened clinicians with a knife (cutting one on the thumb). After numerous consultations, case staffings, and the like, a number of treatment plans had been formulated and eventually defeated. She would call on the telephone several times a day but not speak. When the clinicians attempted to limit the duration of the calls, H. responded by calling 175 times during a single eight-hour shift. The crisis center filed telephone harassment charges against H., but the local magistrate conveniently "forgot" to meet a legal deadline and so was "forced" to drop the charges. The crisis center clinicians then told H. that in lieu of telephoning, she must come in person to the center for help. H. responded by driving her automobile through the glass doors of the building into the waiting room.

Case number 3. S. was a 28-year-old black male chronic schizophrenic inpatient at a state mental hospital. Usually docile, he flushed every toilet on the unit, later made obscene scatological statements to females, and finally struck a female clinician. After the sequence of behaviors had been repeated several times, the clinicians recognized the toilet-flushing as a premonitory sign and began intensive interventions (including medication) at the onset of such behavior. Although S. never was willing to discuss these events, with consistent early intervention further assaults were prevented.

Case number 4. Z. was a strapping 35-year-old white male, well known to the hospital inpatient psychiatric unit personnel. Z. had a reputation as an immature individual who took special delight in setting fires (he also had a fire extinguisher mounted on the back of his motorcycle). Z. was also a notorious bully, who had threatened to strike another male patient and wrapped a leather belt about his fist menacingly when several male clinicians intervened, forming a circle around him as one ordered Z. to the seclusion room. The situation was a volatile standoff until a female clinician (slender and less than five feet tall) came upon the scene without a word. "Peggy!" exclaimed Z., as he dropped his hands and ran to her side; he went peacefully to the seclusion room at her request.

Case number 5.   J. was a 38-year-old white male who had suffered for many years from bipolar disorder and substance abuse. J. had appeared at a local Community Mental Health Center in a psychotic state; he struck one clinician and wandered out into a busy street. Because the center did not have an inpatient unit, the police were called to transport J. to a state psychiatric hospital. Four large officers surrounded J. as the clinician told J. that he would have to go with the officers to the hospital: J. responded with shouted obscenities and threats. The clinician told J. that he could choose whether he wanted to walk to the police car or whether he wanted the officers to carry him. J. responded with further obscenities and threats and said that he chose neither; the clinician told J. that he could finish the cigarette he was smoking (so that J. would not attempt to put it out in someone's face), but that when it was extinguished if he did not get up it would be interpreted as his choice to be carried. When J. finished his smoke, the police took a step forward and J. arose and went to the police car without a struggle.

Case number 6.   While working in her office just outside an inpatient psychiatric unit, J. (the Chief Psychiatric Nurse) heard a sharp inhaling gasp followed by silence. Sensing that something was "not right," she entered the doorway of the inpatient unit and in the adjacent dayroom saw B., a 20-year-old white male, holding a chair aloft about to strike the head of L., another inpatient, who was cowering below in fear. B. had long been the butt of other patients' jokes, and had been mercilessly tormented for several days by L. and others. Holding the chair aloft, B. was crying tears of rage. J. snapped her fingers sharply to get B.'s attention, and she said "Put the chair down and sit on it." As B. quavered, she repeated, "Put the chair down and sit on it" twice more, maintaining eye contact with B. although she did not approach any closer. Finally, slowly,

B. complied as L. ran to safety. When B. sat on the chair, J. said "Okay, now, let's talk about it." B. sobbed in relief. Amazingly, throughout this episode two psychiatric aides had sat oblivious in the same dayroom, watching television: Neither had noticed any of the aforementioned events.

Chapter 6

LEGAL ASPECTS OF PSYCHOLOGICAL/ PHYSICAL CRISIS INTERVENTION

Before turning to a discussion of the physical principles and techniques of crisis intervention, we must first consider the legal context of such interventions. Legal considerations affect the decision to implement interventions, and also affect the choice of intervention method.

OVERVIEW

Many clinicians are understandably uncertain about their legal rights and responsibilities in crises which may require both psychological and physical intervention. Soloff (1984) has noted: "The basic principles of law . . . are easily stated. The permutations of the legal responsibilities that arise in the course of everyday practice, however, are endless and complex" (p. 109). As always, sound judgment will be required in order to integrate and apply such principles as a basis for appropriate practice in concrete situations.

Both patients and clinicians have rights and responsibilities defined by legal standards. There are three sources of these legal standards: (a) statutes generated by local, state, or federal legislature, (b) regulations generated by administrative agencies empowered by the legislature, and (c) case law consisting in precedents set by judicial decisions in similar cases (Appelbaum, 1984). Failure of the patient or of the clinician to meet relevant legal standards can result in crime and/or tort. A crime is an action that is legally prohibited; a tort is a wrongful act resulting in injury to another person (or that person's property) for which that person is entitled to compensation, even though that act might not be illegal. The law may prescribe punishment for crime (imprisonment, fine, restitution, etc.), and financial or other liability may ensue from tort. Negligence, which can be crime and/or tort, is action or inaction amounting to failure to exercise sufficient care for the protection of other persons or their property. Malpractice is professional negligence (Andrade & Andrade, 1979).

Rights and Responsibilities

In general terms, patients have the right to appropriate treatment by the least restrictive methods available, and the right to be protected from harm by clinicians and other patients. Similarly, clinicians have the right to be protected from harm by patients, and to exercise sound professional judgment in providing appropriate emergency treatment.

Appropriate Treatment and the "Standard of Care"

The adequacy and appropriateness of treatment rendered to the patient is defined by the "standard of care," which is the general level of expertise and skill which other professionals deliver (cf. Andrade & Andrade, 1979; Appelbaum, 1984; Creighton, 1979a; Julavits, 1983). The standard of care is specific to the discipline of the clinician. The behavior of a nurse is compared to that of other nurses, that of a physician is compared to that of other physicians, and so on (Andrade & Andrade, 1979). Although in times past the "locality rule" held

that the professional behavior of the clinician would be compared to that of other clinicians in the same community (cf.
Andrade & Andrade, 1979; Creighton, 1979a; Sadoff, 1984),
Julavits (1983) notes that "the legal trend is clearly in the direction of applying national standards" (p. 335). As better training
becomes available, a higher standard of clinical practice becomes the norm ("Liabilities . . .," 1983). From a practical stand-
point, the concept of "standard of care" means that the patient
is entitled to clinical care which utilizes the best of currently
known, commonly available information and technology. Failure of the clinician to provide service consistent with the standard of care places the clinician in legal jeopardy. However,
an unfavorable treatment outcome per se does not necessarily
lead to professional liability so long as the treatment rendered
meets the standard of care (Creighton, 1979a; "Liabilities . . .,"
1983). Negligence has been considered to consist in departure
from the standard of care which adversely affects the patient
(Andrade & Andrade, 1979; Appelbaum, 1983, 1984; Sadoff,
1984).

   Written standards.   Written standards do not always exist
nor are they always appropriate; however, the clinician is probably best protected when clearly acting in accordance with a
reasonable, explicit written standard. Every agency and institution should have a written policy regarding the procedures for
proper management of violent emergency situations (cf. Guirguis, 1978; Guirguis & Durost, 1978; Kronberg, 1983; Nigrosh,
1983; Penningroth, 1975; Rosen & DiGiacomo, 1978). Such a
written policy can enhance the quality of clinical care by out-
lining accepted procedures and alternatives, delegating authority appropriately, clarifying expectations, and specifying roles
and functions. There is certainly resistance to formulating a
written policy for the management of violent emergencies. Some
agencies seem to ignore the reality of aggressive behavior, and
some clinicians seem to fear that they will be held to an unrealistic expectation. However, a written policy may also actually protect the clinician and the agency. In the event of an
untoward intervention outcome, one is probably in the best
possible position when one has acted in accordance with rea-

sonable, previously approved guidelines. In contrast, one is vulnerable when violating written guidelines without clear justification, or when performing common procedures in absence of a written policy (one might be considered deficient by virtue of not having written standards for common procedures). While the particulars of any written procedures must be tailored to the unique characteristics, circumstances, philosophy, and values of the individual agency and clinicians, the following are points which should be considered:

1. Overall responsibility to formulate guidelines and procedures should be vested in a standing interdisciplinary committee, if possible, with representatives from public and patient sectors; representatives from each clinical discipline; and representatives from related services such as administration, chaplaincy, legal, public relations, and security. In addition to producing written policy, such a committee should oversee and approve intervention methods and training programs, and should have a designated subcommittee to meet on a regular basis to review violent incidents and to serve as a mechanism for hearing both patient and clinician grievances regarding the handling or policy for violent emergencies.

2. The necessity of exercising clinical judgment and of considering intervention methods in light of the relevant circumstances should be acknowledged. Explicit agency support should be stated for clinicians acting in good faith according to guidelines presented. This support should include appropriate legal representation when necessary.

3. Rights and responsibilities of both clinicians and patients should be specified. Clinicians must have the right to take necessary measures to protect themselves, other patients, and property, yet must not be required to subject themselves to risk of serious bodily harm: Clinicians must have the right to defer physical intervention until sufficient numbers of backup personnel are available. Patients must have the right to be free from mistreatment by clinicians and by other patients. Abuse should be defined, and clinician responsibility to refrain from abusing patients and clinician responsibility to report suspected abuse must be explicit. Patients must be required to conduct themselves appropriately within the limits of their ability to do

so. Methods for addressing patient and clinician grievances and for patient and clinician discipline must be specified.

4. Purposes of and indications/contraindications for initiating/terminating specific methods of intervention (e.g., seclusion, restraint, medication) and the expectation for due consideration of least-restrictive alternatives should be specified. Requirements for periodic or continuous patient monitoring during emergency seclusion and restraint must be stated, as must a protocol for rapid neuroleptization.

5. Examples of approved intervention methods should be presented (a training manual or videotape may prove to be a useful appendix for this part of the written procedure). Approval of the emergency use of physical intervention, including intervention in order to prevent anticipated violence, should be explicit. A protocol for team interventions such as seclusion and mechanical restraint (including determination of leadership, decision-making authority, follow-up procedures such as debriefing, etc.) should be included.

6. Procedures and requirements for clinician training (including who is and who is not required to undergo training and periodic retraining), for instructor certification, and for curriculum approval should be specified.

7. Requirements for the architectural safety of the clinical setting should be specified, including the design of seclusion rooms, the inclusion of emergency distress devices for clinicians, etc.

8. Agency support, guidelines, and procedures for pursuing civil and/or criminal legal action against patients and for transfer, therapeutic discharge, etc., should be stated.

9. Roles should be delineated between various professions, such as clinicians, security officers, et al., and procedures for mustering sufficient backup personnel specified. Responsibility for determining intervention strategy and methods must be stated. Among clinical staff, those with authority to order emergency seclusion, mechanical restraint, and medication must be specified.

10. Requirements and criteria for documentation of episodes of violent behavior, and for follow-up notification of appropriate agency personnel should be made explicit.

11. Procedures for "violence precautions" regarding patients known or suspected to be at risk for violent actions should be specified, including methods of early identification of such patients and for dissemination of precautions.

Documentation.   In addition to the actual clinical procedures implemented, the clinician is required to document the procedures appropriately; inadequate record keeping can in itself be considered a substandard practice (cf. Julavits, 1983). Because emergency situations cannot all be reasonably anticipated and because the ultimate effects of interventions chosen during an emergency cannot always be foreseen, special attention to careful documentation is essential (cf. Dix, in press). The clinical record is often admissible as legal evidence (cf. Creighton, 1979c). The clinical record must be complete, factual, and scrupulously honest. The clinician must not misstate nor omit facts which indicate that the clinician may have committed an error in procedure or judgment—the documentation of such errors attest to the honesty and integrity of the record, and may protect the clinician from untrue allegations which could be even worse than any actual shortcomings. Falsification of records (including falsification by omission) can lead to civil and criminal liability (Creighton, 1978). Incident reports notoriously underreport the true prevalence of violence because staff fear supervisory disapproval for reporting and because there is often no consensus regarding what constitutes a reportable incident (cf. Adler, Kreeger & Ziegler, 1983; Conn & Lion, 1983; Lion, Snyder & Merrill, 1981; Piercy, 1984); however, insurance carriers may not have to cover a case for which an incident report was not properly executed (cf. Creighton, 1979b). The clinician should avoid speculation in the clinical record (cf. Creighton, 1979b).

The following points have been noted for inclusion in the clinical record (e.g., Dix, in press; Julavits, 1983; Piercy, 1984); a special incident reporting form may help to ensure:

1.   Creation of the record at or near the time that the incident occurred by someone with firsthand experi-

ence of the incident, and with signatures of all staff involved.

2. The date, place, location, full names of all persons (both
   patients and staff) involved and witnesses.
3. Behavioral description of incident, including appearance, demeanor, statements, actions/reactions, precipitants, and other relevant focal or contextual factors.
4. Complete description of facts that·caused clinician to
   consider the situation an emergency, rationale for choice
   of intervention method (including explicit discussion
   of less restrictive alternatives considered and reasons
   for rejecting each), specific criteria for implementation
   of less intensive intervention (e.g., release from restraint), and steps taken to prevent another similar incident.
5. Exact time and duration of intervention (e.g., manual
   or mechanical restraint, seclusion), description of care
   given during intervention (e.g., vital sign monitoring,
   toileting), time of notification of other appropriate professionals (e.g., physician contact), and other appropriate follow-up action (e.g., incident review).
6. Complete description of property damaged and of injuries suffered by patient and clinician: If trauma is
   visible, color photographs should be taken.

Ultimately, "reasonableness in light of circumstances" will
be the standard by which the quality and appropriateness of
clinical care in any given instance will be evaluated. The clinician is always required to employ sound judgment in implementing clinical interventions, the customary "standard of care"
and written procedures notwithstanding (Appelbaum, 1983).
However, the clinician must realize that juries may find a simple error in judgment "indistinguishable from the most clear
cut negligence" (Appelbaum, 1984, p. 102). Therefore, as a
legal protection and (more important) as a clinical validation,
the clinician should whenever possible consult with colleagues
in important matters requiring judgment and document the
consultation appropriately (Appelbaum, 1983, 1984; Dix, in

press). Such consultation demonstrates the clinician's intention to deliver quality care, and may even be required by the standard of care.

"Least Restrictive Alternative"

The "least restrictive alternative" for adequate treatment has proven difficult to define and to apply to actual clinical situations. Rather than representing a unidimensional continuum from the least restrictive to the most restrictive treatment methods, "relative restrictiveness" is actually a multidimensional construct. Whether a given treatment method is relatively more or relatively less restrictive than an alternative may be a function of each method's behavioral intrusiveness, physical intrusiveness, effectiveness, reversibility, safety, painfulness; effect upon the patient's dignity and responsibility; treatment setting; whether the treatment is voluntary or involuntary; etc. (cf. Bachrach, 1980; Killebrew, Harris & Kruckeberg, 1982; Kloss, 1980; Ransohoff, Zachary, Gaynor & Hargreaves, 1982). There is no consensus among legal experts as to the relative restrictiveness of involuntary procedures involving medication, seclusion, and mechanical restraint. Although perhaps counterintuitive, some experts argue that medication may be more restrictive than even mechanical restraint because medication is invasive; others argue that seclusion may be more restrictive than mechanical restraint because seclusion restricts access to socialization; etc. (cf. Dix, in press; Gertz, 1980; Gutheil, Appelbaum & Wexler, 1983). In the applied situation, while the clinician must be mindful of the requirements for implementing the least restrictive treatment, the decision as to actual method of intervention cannot be made on a priori grounds but rather must be made with respect to the individual patient and the particulars of the situation and possible treatment approaches (cf. Ransohoff, 1980; Switzsky & Miller, 1978).

Emergency Measures

Patients have a general right to be free from involuntary treatment (unless, of course, an individual patient's rights have been specifically abridged); however, in emergency situations requiring immediate action the clinician has substantial authority and responsibility to take necessary action (such as physical intervention, medication, seclusion, and restraint) to protect the patient, the self, and others (cf. Appelbaum, 1984; Dix, in press; Soloff, Gutheil & Wexler, 1985; Wexler, 1984). Behavior which is destructive to the patient, to others, or to the therapeutic environment legally warrants immediate involuntary intervention; similarly, preventive intervention when such destructive behaviors appear to be imminent but have not actually occurred (even in absence of a specific threat or act) is considered legally appropriate (Appelbaum, 1983; Dix, in press; Gutheil, 1978; Sadoff, 1984; Soloff, 1982; Wexler, 1982). In an emergency situation, the clinician is given a great deal of flexibility in applying judgment to determine the necessity of and particular methods of immediate intervention. The clinician's judgment will be presumed to be valid, and the clinician will be liable only if the intervention performed is such a substantial departure from the usual standard of care that it calls into question whether judgment was in fact exercised at all (Soloff, Gutheil & Wexler, 1985; Wexler, 1984).

Right to Protection

By virtue of the patient-clinician relationship, the patient has a right to be protected from harm resulting from the actions of the clinician, from the actions of other patients, and even from the patient's own actions (Appelbaum, 1983; Schwab & Lahmeyer, 1979; Soloff, 1983): The clinician must exercise reasonable care in order not to harm the patient; the clinician must protect the patient from other patients; and the clinician must supervise and even restrain the patient from self-harm when necessary. Failure to protect the patient may result in criminal or tort liability for the clinician (cf. Taitz, 1984).

Assault is an attempt or threat to do violence against another person, regardless of whether the attempt or threat is actually carried out. Battery is an actual, unlawful attack upon another person. Even touching the person's clothing, or an object held by the person, can constitute battery. Both clinicians and patients can be guilty of assault and/or battery. Abuse is maltreatment of a patient, and can be crime and/or tort consisting in acts of omission as well as acts of commission. There are many varieties of abuse. Physical abuse may consist in bodily mistreatment such as striking, rough handling, and inflicting injury or pain; psychological abuse may consist in verbal or nonverbal actions such as demeaning or humiliating words or demeanor, exploitation, coercion, or threat; other abuse may consist in neglect or failure of the clinician to take therapeutic action, failure to protect the patient, and failure to report abuse by another clinician (cf. Creighton, 1976; Nations, 1973; Snyder, 1983).

Clinicians also have a right to be free from unreasonable harm by patients (Appelbaum, 1983). As Rachlin (1982) stated: "Perhaps the largest area of concern relates to who takes what amount of abuse from whom" (p. 60). The major difference between the clinician's private response to aggressive behavior in a nonclinical situation and the behavior required in the clinical setting is that in the latter case, the clinician's actions will be judged by quality-of-care criteria: Care and treatment of the patient are always a consideration, even when the clinician is justifiably protecting the self. The clinician has a right and responsibility to use reasonable force in the course of therapeutic physical intervention involving patient control and/or self-protection (cf. Allison & Bale, 1973; Creighton, 1976, 1982; Nations, 1973; Nigrosh, 1983; Snyder, 1983; Soloff, 1979); failure to use sufficient, reasonable force in order to prevent one patient from harming another patient may make the clinician liable (Appelbaum, 1983; "Psychiatric Emergencies: Update," 1980; "Restraining . . . ," 1982). Of course, even in response to extreme patient provocation, the use of excessive force is intolerable ("Abusive Patients . . .," 1982) whether in the course of legitimate self-protection (Creighton, 1982) or otherwise. As Snyder (1983) has written, "The desired tone of the staff's behavior . . . should be defensive rather than aggressive, controlling rather than punitive, and with no more forcefulness than the situation requires" (p. 159); yet the amount of force that is considered appropriate will remain a matter of judgment, dependent upon the context of the specific persons and situation involved. Two extreme examples, each involving the death of a psychiatric patient, are worth recounting. In one case, an institution and clinicians were successfully sued when a fleeing, agitated patient was tackled by a physician and a nurse. In order to restrain the patient, the physician placed a tourniquet about the patient's neck and emptied a container of ether into the patient's face ("Psychiatric Emergencies: Update," 1980). In the other case, a patient assaulted a nurse and in the course of restraint the patient struggled violently and was inadvertently choked; although the nurse was initially convicted of criminally negligent homicide, the state Supreme Court overturned the conviction on the basis that the death was unintentional and the patient could not be adequately controlled without holding the patient's neck ("Restraining . . .," 1982). In the first case, force was unreasonable and excessive; in the second case, though the outcome was tragic, the amount of force was held to be reasonable because a lesser degree of force would have been unlikely to protect the clinician or other patients. The jursiprudent clinician must be prepared to prove that any degree of force (whether for protection of the patient or of the self) was *not* unreasonable.

In years past, the judicial tendency may have been to consider patients as not responsible for their aggressive conduct within the clinical setting; however, contemporary legal thinking seems to hold that unless the patient's capacity to do so is substantially compromised by major mental disability, the patient is legally required to conform to standards of behavior expected of other members of society ("Patient Behavior . . .," 1981), and clinicians technically have the right to sue patients for damage resulting from conscious, willful aggression ("Assaults . . .," 1981; Kronberg, 1983; Sales, Overcast & Merrikin, 1983) and to file criminal charges when appropriate (Lion, Snyder & Merrill, 1981; Perry & Gilmore, 1981). However, in practice a lawsuit against an aggressive patient may prove difficult as some courts have cited an "assumption of risk" by clinicians by virtue of their employment (cf. Creighton, 1982; Nigrosh, 1983). Likewise, prosecution of the mental patient is complex and fraught with both clinical and pragmatic difficulties (Gutheil, 1985; Mills, Phelan & Ryan, 1985). Prosecutors are likely to be unenthusiastic about pursuing such cases and lay juries are apt to be sympathetic to the patient (Appelbaum, 1983; "Liabilities . . .," 1983). However, for certain patients civil and/or criminal proceedings may be expedient and therapeutic in that the patient is given the clear message of the inappropriateness of assaultive or destructive behavior (cf. Appelbaum, 1983; Gutheil & Rivinus, 1982; Schwartz & Greenfield, 1978): Such action will, of course, require close coordination with the police and the courts (Phelan, Mills & Ryan, 1985; Stein & Diamond, 1985). Workers Compensation is also a viable option for the clinician who is physically or psychologically injured in the course of professional work ("Assaults . . .," 1981; Sales, Overcast & Merrikin, 1983).

Discharge from professional care is also an option to be considered for some aggressive patients. Like taking legal action against a patient, "therapeutic discharge" is a complex procedure. For some patients, treatment actually produces deterioration in functioning, and when this deterioration takes the form of aggressive acting out, discharge should be considered (cf. Appelbaum, 1983; Friedman, 1969); at times, such a discharge may make the patient more amenable to subsequent treatment by another clinician or in another setting (cf. Crabtree, 1982; Friedman, 1969). One must be mindful, however, of responsibilities to others and should an aggressive patient be likely to harm others upon discharge, then a transfer to jail or to another mental health facility may be preferable to outright release (cf. Appelbaum, 1983; Creighton, 1982; Gutheil, 1978). Decisions concerning therapeutic discharge should be made in terms of the patient's clinical picture rather than the clinician's emotional reactions to the assault. Criteria for discharging patients should be identified early in treatment and should be defined clearly (Penna, 1983).

CONCLUSION

Both the patient and the clinician have rights and responsibilities in the therapeutic setting. The patient has the right to appropriate, least restrictive treatment, and the right to be free from harm; the clinician has the right to protect the self from the patient, and the right to intervene in an emergency. Both the patient and the clinician may be criminally and/or civilly responsible for their actions. Judgment is central to the evaluation of the actions of both the patient and of the clinician.

The clinician must know the general principles which relate to the legal aspects of professional mental health practice, and should strive "to integrate legal considerations into an appropriate plan of clinical care" (Appelbaum, 1984, p. 101). Ultimately, decisions about the patient should be made on clinical grounds (Julavits, 1983; Perry & Gilmore, 1981; Rachlin, 1982): Actions which make the most clinical sense will typically be best for both patient and clinician.

Chapter 7

PRINCIPLES OF PHYSICAL INTERVENTION

PSYCHOLOGICAL ORIENTATION

Physical intervention principles conceptually intersect with psychological principles. Applied physical techniques are effective only insofar as they utilize psychological as well as mechanical/kinesiological principles. Aggressive behavior is a meaningful event for both the patient and for the clinician.

Of course, sound judgment is the ultimate basis for determining the best psychological intervention, and sound judgment is likewise required of the clinician in order to implement the proper physical intervention. There is not a concrete physical response for each possible situation. Instead, the clinician must apply identified principles to the situation at hand. As with psychological principles, there are rules for physical intervention yet no overriding rule to determine which specific rule to follow at any given moment. The clinician must judge the necessity of physical intervention and also judge its specific implementation and procedure. As Gair (1980) has noted: "Indications for physical intervention can never be entirely definitive, since the most significant determinants require personal judgment at the time" (p. 16).

An understanding of principles underlying the techniques of intervention is more important than rote memorization of maneuvers; therefore a comprehensive discussion of these principles will be undertaken before presentation of their concrete applications. Principles underlying physical intervention are summarized in table 4.

Table 4.   Principles Underlying Physical Intervention

Psychological preparation of the clinician
    Appreciate realistic limitations
    Have sense of sacrifice
    Avoid desperation
    Perform in serial order
    Utilize proper timing
Actions and reactions of the patient
    Anticipate patient actions and reactions
Mechanical/kinesiological factors
    Avoid danger zone
    Utilize appropriate stance
    Protect head and throat
    Do not oppose force
    Deflect
    Pivot
    Control patient's hand
    Induce weak position
    Apply torque
    Utilize anaerobic cycle
    Utilize body weight
    Wedge
    Utilize leverage
    Hold at joint
    Bend elbow to strengthen, straighten to weaken

Psychological Preparation of the Clinician

Appreciate realistic limitations.   The clinician must have reasonable expectations regarding what is and is not possible. Although protection and control can indeed be accomplished, no amount of physical training will allow a clinician to intervene *easily* with a much larger patient. The clinician must be sensitive to both psychological and physical aspects of the situation and relevant limiting factors; the clinician must know when to stay and when to leave, when to go it alone and when to ask for help.

Have sense of sacrifice.   The clinician must acknowledge that any physical intervention will have its price. A sense of appropriate sacrifice is essential. One may sustain bumps, bruises, and strains in preference to permanent injury; and one may suffer permanent injury to escape death. A personal psychological toll must not be underestimated. Emotional recovery from an incident is typically measured in terms of months rather than minutes.

Avoid desperation.   The clinician must expect to have an emotional reaction at the first instant of attack. Most clinicians will perhaps feel a momentary flash of panic. However, the clinician need not "react to the reaction" and complicate the matter by concluding that a personal loss of control has occurred; rather, the clinician learns that, following such an initial shock, recovery and ability to focus upon the task at hand will eventually ensue.

Perform in serial order.   The clinician must not attempt to perform all aspects of a complex intervention simultaneously, but rather should become accustomed to thinking about sophisticated tasks in terms of elemental subroutines which are executed in serial order, one step at a time. The clinician will feel more capable psychologically and will perform better physically when addressing small components sequentially.

Utilize proper timing.   At times the clinician's best possible response to a physical situation is simply to *wait* and defer an attempt at physical intervention. The clinician may instead attempt to negotiate with the patient, ask to be released, etc. Of course, the clinician can utilize such a period of watchful waiting to think, and to choose carefully the appropriate time for swift and precipitous action. At times the clinician can avoid the patient's concentrated resistance by implementing a defense, escape, or control sequence so quickly that the patient does not have sufficient time to resist the clinician's actions: Some techniques can actually be executed faster than the patient's reactive reflex time (cf. Choi, 1975). Acting swiftly may not necessarily mean that the clinician will attempt a physical maneuver at the first instant of a patient attack; rather, this principle implies that when the clinician finds an appropriate instant the technique is implemented swiftly and without allowing the patient to anticipate the action.

Actions and Reactions of the Patient

Anticipate patient actions and reactions.   The clinician must anticipate the actions of the patient. Some attacks can be adequately addressed only through prevention. No amount of sheer physical training or prowess will allow one to defend against the completely unexpected "sucker punch," knife attack, or shooting. One must use psychological skills to assess the patient, the self, and the situation in order to anticipate the patient's actions so as to prevent or to interrupt aggressive behavior. The patient's reactions are also a primary consideration affecting choice of intervention procedure. The clinician can avoid inadvertently precipitating an attack by being sensitive to the patient's likely reaction; for example, a patient may strike out at the clinician who encroaches upon the patient's body-buffer zone. At times the patient's reaction can be utilized as an integral part of a defense, escape, or control sequence. At times the clinician must actively divert the patient's attention in order to gain the opportunity for physical intervention. With such distraction the patient is less able to anticipate and oppose the clinician's actions through increased force, resistance, and aggression.

Mechanical Kinesiological Factors

Avoid danger zone. The patient is typically able to move most quickly and forcefully toward the front; the patient can attack less easily toward the side, and can attack toward the rear only with difficulty. Therefore the clinician should avoid the front of the patient, and should instead stay to one side of or behind the patient. Three zones can be conceptualized as surrounding the patient (as shown in figure 6): (a) the "distal safety zone" which is farther than the patient can precipitously lunge,

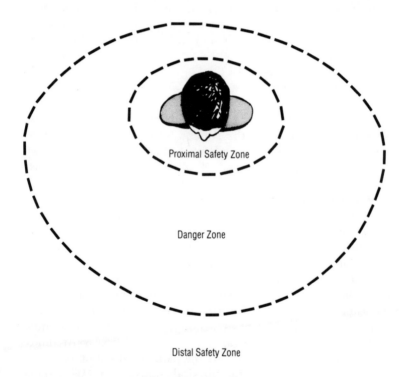

Figure 6.   **Danger Zones and Safety Zones (overhead view).**

punch, or kick, (b) the "danger zone" which is within striking distance, and (c) the "proximal safety zone" which is too close for the patient to effectively deliver strikes. In some maneuvers the clinician will attempt to remain within the distal safety zone, and in other maneuvers the clinician will attempt to remain within the proximal safety zone. The clinician must be careful to avoid inadvertently entering or remaining within the danger zone.

Utilize appropriate stance. Strength, balance, and mobility require that the clinician keep the knees slightly bent rather than locked straight, that the weight be distributed mainly over the balls of the feet rather than over the heels, and that the feet remain about one shoulder's width apart (closer together is relatively unstable and farther apart is relatively immobile). The stance is strongest along an imaginary straight line drawn through both feet (coronal plane) and is weakest perpendicular to that line (midsaggital plane). These aspects are shown in figure 7. Standing sideways toward the patient utilizes the strongest dimension of the stance; standing sideways also permits the clinician to lean sideways (away from the patient) faster and farther than the clinician would be able to lean in a backward direction when facing the patient frontally. In lifting, the clinician's feet should be spread slightly wider than the usual shoulder width, the knees should be bent and the spine kept as nearly vertical as possible. Lifting power should be generated from the clinician's thigh muscles rather than with the back. Controlled, slow exhalation is sometimes helpful.

Protect head and throat. The head is the most sensitive to impact of all bodily vital spots. For both the clinician and the patient, protection of the head from impact must be a primary consideration. The neck is the most sensitive to constriction of all bodily vital spots because it is essential for the continuous flow of blood and air. Protection of the clinician's and the patient's throat is essential.

Do not oppose force. Whenever possible, the clinician should not oppose the patient's force. The clinician should at-

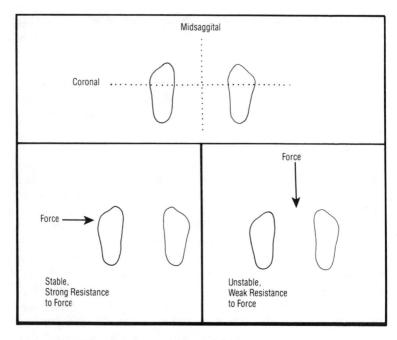

**Figure 7.   Dimensions of relative strength and weakness
in stance (overhead view).**

tempt to move in an alternative direction if strongly opposed
by the patient.

Deflect.   An attack must sometimes be intercepted with a
nonvital body part (such as arm or leg) or with an object; ideally
this deflection should be applied obliquely rather than squarely
against the vector of attack. A superior strategy is to have a
"checking block" already in place which inhibits the initiation
of an attack, rather than attempting to intercept an attack in
midflight. For example, a patient's punch cannot be cleanly or
forcefully executed when the clinician's hand already rests upon
the patient's arm, thus smothering the attack or guiding it away
from the intended target. As illustrated in figure 8, the clinician's hands move from head level downward toward the mid-

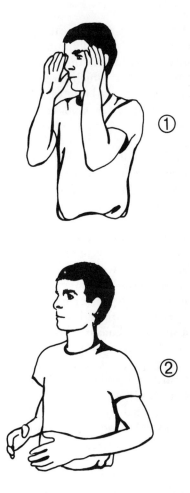

Figure 8. The hands move more quickly and forcefully from position 1 toward position 2 than vice versa.

section much more forcefully and rapidly than they can move from the midsection upward toward the head. Therefore, many blocking motions begin with at least one hand high so that the clinician's head can be safely protected, and if necessary can be lowered quickly to protect the torso.

Pivot.   Because the patient can move forward toward the clinician much more forcefully and quickly than the clinician can retreat directly backward, the superior avoidance maneuver entails a circular evasion which moves the clinician out of the patient's attack vector. Variants of this procedure are shown in figure 9. Pivoting is fast and leaves the clinician oriented obliquely to the patient's attack vector.

Control patient's hand.   Grabbing attacks by the patient can be injurious because the patient can shake, tear, or twist the captured body part. The clinician must establish control over the grabbing hand as a priority.

Induce weak position.   Movements have points of maximum and minimal mechanical efficiency. For example, the patient's grabbing action with the palm downward is strongest when applied well above the patient's waist, and is weakest when applied below the waist; conversely, the palm-up grabbing motion is strongest when applied low, and weakest when applied high. Obviously, the clinician should attempt to position the patient into a relatively weak position. The thumb is the weakest part of the grip. In contrast to the several fingers which are curled inward and prehensile, the single thumb curves outward and is relatively weak, ill suited for grabbing. Also, the thumb adducts toward the fingers with more strength than it abducts. In many releasing and object-removal procedures, the "rule of thumb" is to oppose it!

Apply torque.   Torque is a rotating, twisting action which can be very difficult to grasp or to oppose. Torquing motions are used in many escape sequences.

Utilize anaerobic cycle.   Focused spurts of intense exertion cannot be maintained; such force, rather, has wavelike peaks and valleys of intensity over time (cf. Katch & McArdle, 1977). Ideally, the clinician should allow the patient to tire, and intervene during the period of the patient's anaerobic depletion rather than at the peak of the patient's strength. The clinician should act during the clinician's time of peak anaerobic poten-

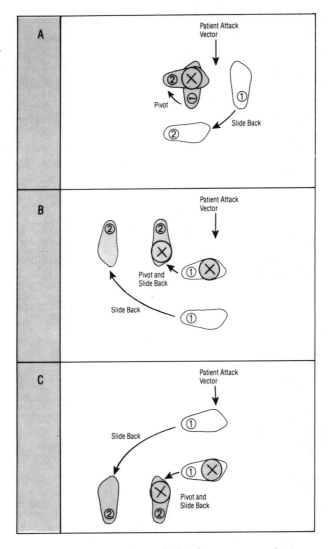

Figure 9.   Three variants of pivoting maneuver (overhead view): (a) pivot on either from frontal
position off to one side; (b) pivot on the forward foot from sideways position; (c) pivot on
rear foot from sideways position.

tial, and should time maneuvers to coincide with the patient's time of minimal power.

Utilize body weight.   The clinician can use both the clinician's and the patient's body weight in lieu of muscle power in effecting both escape and control procedures. Effective use of body weight will tire the patient rather than the clinician.

Wedge.   Some releases must be effected in a series of small increments which gradually create an opening, just as a wedge gradually splits a log. Wedging is especially useful when the patient is much stronger than the clinician.

Utilize leverage.   Mechanical advantage can be gained by utilizing leverage. For example, the clinician can more easily move a patient's arm sideways by pushing near the wrist rather than near the shoulder.

Hold at joint.   The large joints (e.g., shoulders, elbows, hips, knees) are the safest and most mechanically efficient points at which to grasp the patient for purposes of control and restraint.

Bend elbow to strengthen, straighten to weaken.   The clinician's arm can generally exert far more force when bent at the elbow rather than straightened. Additionally, as shown in figure 10, the crook of the elbow is far superior to the hand for lifting because the force of the load is not levered. The patient's arm is weakest when straightened (this position also affords greatest leverage potential). Because arms adduct with more force than they abduct, their point of minimum strength is reached when they are straightened and drawn completely across the chest. This is the "straitjacket" position, used in nonmechanical as well as mechanical restraint positions.

APPLYING THE PRINCIPLES

The principles of physical intervention must be translated by the clinician into the applied procedures for physical inter-

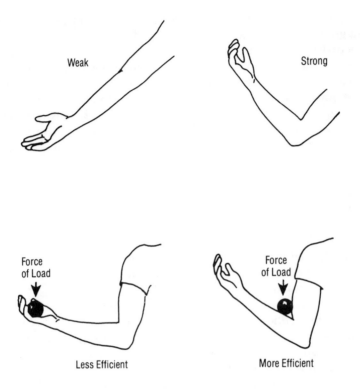

Figure 10. The arm is weak when straight, strong when bent at the elbow; a load is most efficiently lifted in the crook of the elbow rather than in the hand.

vention. Various alternatives for physical intervention in prototypical situations will be presented, yet in any actual physical intervention the clinician will have to use sound judgment in choosing among possible approaches. The clinician must know what is realistic, and expect that an actual physical intervention cannot be accurately mirrored during practice sessions. Even if one were to practice at "full force and fury," the psychological factors which underlie actual assault against the clinician would not be present. However, it is reasonable to analyze actual physical interventions in terms of basic components. For example, the clinician may learn various ways to protect against a grab, to protect against a punch, and to effect restraint. In an actual situation, the clinician may very well have to integrate several different maneuvers in order to deal with a complex situation, perhaps one in which the patient first grabs and then begins to punch the clinician. The clinician may therefore have to select the optimal procedure for protection against grabbing and combine it with protection against punching, and then decide whether to attempt restraint, to attempt escape, or perhaps even to seize upon an opportunity to attempt further verbal/nonverbal therapeutic intervention with the patient. The possibilities are myriad; therefore, rather than attempt to portray a specific response to each and every eventuality, a modular set of maneuvers for dealing with the more common components of physical intervention demands will be presented, and the clinician can choose among, combine, and alter the maneuvers according to the particulars of the patient, the clinician, and the situation.

Of course, the emphasis in physical intervention is always upon prevention, with the use of least restrictive methods consistent with sound care and treatment of the patient. Physical altercations are to be resolved, never won; volatile situations must always be handled at the lowest possible level of escalation. Inasmuch as assaultive behavior is meaningful to both patient and clinician, every attempt must be made to preserve communication and to address the meaning of the patient's behavior, both as a pragmatic issue necessary for effecting control and as a therapeutic issue necessary for effecting treatment. The treatment milieu is a social matrix, with a subculture that is influenced by and which in turn influences both patients and clinicians (Penna, 1983). The milieu must be safe to be therapeutic; and although angry verbal expression is often appropriate, a proscription against overt physical violence is necessary. The clinician must not hesitate to make such behavioral expectations an explicit and regular part of initial patient interviewing, community meetings, and the like; and any occurrence of violent behavior must be discussed as a community issue that affects the milieu as a whole rather than merely the immediate participants (cf. Felthous, 1984).

CRITERIA FOR ACCEPTABLE PHYSICAL TECHNIQUES

The clinician needs a repertoire of professional physical techniques for self-preservation and patient control which are consistent with the overall purpose of crisis intervention. These techniques must facilitate therapeutic psychological intervention while protecting both the clinician and patient from injury. Such techniques must meet a number of essential criteria:

1. The techniques must be realistically effective. Rather than an amalgam of discrete, concrete interventions for specific applications, physical intervention can and should be conceptualized in terms of general principles which will allow the clinician to adapt the response to the demands of complex, novel situations.

2. The techniques must be safe for clinician and patient alike. The clinician must be adequately protected, and the procedures should be "forgiving" of flaws in technical execution. Techniques which can leave the clinician in an unsafe, untenable position in the event of a technical error are inadequate. Likewise, the techniques must not jeopardize the patient's safety either directly or as a result of deficiency in the clinician's technique.

3. The techniques must be absolutely nonabusive. The techniques must preserve the humanity and dignity of the patient; they must allow responses which are appropriately graduated in terms of relative restrictiveness, intrusiveness, and forcefulness. Techniques must not depend upon the induction of pain nor upon orthopedically unsound limb positioning for their efficacy. Because of the different purpose of mental health practice, the technology of therapeutic physical crisis intervention will necessarily be different from that employed by correctional, police, or security functionaries.

4. The techniques must require an absolute minimum of clinician training and practice for adequate proficiency. Most clinicians understandably have little interest in physical intervention skills training per se, and none should need to develop unusual physical abilities in order to become professionally competent. Ideally, techniques should be similar to learning to ride a bicycle—a skill that, once learned, is retained indefinitely.

Realistically, periodic practice is usually required to maintain physical intervention skills, but techniques should not require intensive training to acquire nor constant rehearsal to retain. The techniques should be integrated into the clinical setting, and tailored to the limitations that an organization may place upon devoting scarce resources to such staff education. The kinds of techniques focused upon should reflect the demands of the therapeutic environment (e.g., special emphasis upon restraining procedures in an emergency department, or upon secluding procedures in an inpatient unit). While the nature of the clinical situation at some institutions may necessitate constant physical skills practice to maintain a necessarily fine-tuned level of intervention expertise (e.g., drug-free observation/evaluation units for research on violent behavior), for most settings this degree of emphasis on physical skills will not be necessary. Techniques should be simple enough to be effectively accessed during the anxiety and confusion of a violent emergency situation.

For the most part, there is agreement among writers in the literature as to the principles and techniques of psychological intervention. With relatively minor differences, most authors emphasize similar points. In sharp contrast, however, is the disagreement concerning acceptable systems and methods of physical intervention. This state of affairs has come about for three main reasons. First, there are differences in fundamental assumptions about the purpose of physical intervention. Second, there are differences of opinion regarding the requirements for adequate physical contact skills training (cf. Nigrosh, 1983). Third, physical intervention technology has actually evolved over the past few years. Although early technology consisted primarily in unsystematized, specific maneuvers immediately derived from police tactics and the martial arts, more recent developments have systematically addressed the principles underlying the technology, and have eliminated aspects which might be appropriate in a different setting but which must be considered abusive or otherwise unacceptable in professional mental health practice. Adherents of particular (especially proprietary) systems are apt to make claims for the efficacy of their approach which go substantially beyond the demonstrable facts.

The clinician is advised to beware of promises of "secret techniques" which can enable a small clinician to easily control a larger patient. When sufficiently agitated, even a small patient can become quite dangerous and difficult for even the large, skilled clinician to manage. There really are no "secrets": Essentially, physical intervention techniques are effective because the clinician (a) is psychologically prepared, (b) utilizes the actions and reactions of the patient, and (c) is able to apply mechanical/kinesiological principles which take maximal advantage of the clinician's own strength and body position relative to that of the patient.

The principles and techniques to be presented in this volume meet all four of the essential criteria presented above; for the most part these principles and techniques represent an eclectic sampling and integration of contemporary practices in the field. Because such practices continue to evolve, the present material is better considered a provisional rather than a definitive statement. Techniques presented elsewhere may also meet the four essential criteria. Procedures presented here can be considered a reasonable benchmark, and the practitioner must judge the merit of alternative approaches and newer developments by the standard of the four essential criteria, and the relative efficacy of different approaches to physical intervention. Finally, training in the actual physical techniques should ideally be undertaken under knowledgeable professional supervision.

Chapter 8

PHYSICAL TECHNIQUES FOR
SELF-PRESERVATION

PREVENTION AND MANAGEMENT OF COMMON ATTACKS

Although there are endless varieties of possible attacks, they can be conceptually and practically dichotomized into *strikes* and *grabs*. Of course, prevention is to be emphasized. Lacking prevention, however, the general defense against strikes is *deflection/blocking of the attacking object* and the general defense against grabs is *controlling of the patient's grabbing hand(s)*.

Nonthreatening Protected Posture

The Nonthreatening Protected Posture is adopted when the clinician wants to avoid making the patient feel threatened, and anticipates that the patient might attempt to punch, kick, or strike the clinician with a held or a thrown object. This posture places the clinician in the best possible position to protect the self from an actual attack. Two variants of the Nonthreatening Protected Posture are shown in figures 11 and 12. In the Nonthreatening Protected Posture, the clinician maintains a sideways posture, and (as naturally as possible) keeps the hands

Figures 11 and 12.   Two variants of the Nonthreatening
Protected Posture.

and arms ready for rapid self-protective movement. The clinician takes care to stay well within the Distal Safety Zone (beyond the Danger Zone), slightly to one side of rather than directly in front of the patient. In addition to nonthreatening verbalizations and paraverbalizations, the clinician communicates nonthreatening kinesic and proxemic messages. Crowding, sudden movements, and inadvertently threatening gestures are avoided. Because of the margin of physical safety afforded by this posture, the clinician may feel realistically able to work with a crisis despite the tension of the situation; alternatively, the clinician may need to leave the situation.

Against Punch, Kick, and Related Attacks

The clinician absolutely must anticipate a punch, kick, or similar attack because the completely unanticipated attack may travel faster than even the most rapid human reaction time (cf. Choi, 1975). In addition to other verbal and nonverbal signs, the clinician should pay particular attention to the patient's eyes. The patient will typically look at the intended target of an attack (e.g., at the head or midsection for a punch, and at the groin or abdomen for a kick). Gaze is an index of intention; the patient might glance at an object before grabbing it to use as a weapon. Knowing the patient's intentions in this way can help the clinician to prevent or minimize the effects of an attack. Of course, one possibility is to anticipate an attack and to stay in the Distal Safety Zone, far enough away so that the patient is unable to make contact with a punch or kick. Alternatively, the clinician may enter the Proximal Safety Zone, so close to the patient that an effective punch or kick is not possible. In such a case, the clinician may also utilize a "checking block" as shown in figures 13 and 14. The checking block smothers an attack or guides it away so that it cannot be delivered effectively. Checking blocks are especially effective as preventive procedures, to be used before an attack has begun. When the clinician is not able to move into either the Distal Safety Zone or the Proximal Safety Zone, the clinician must deflect or block the attack with the arms, legs, or an appropriate object (depending upon the particulars of the attack).

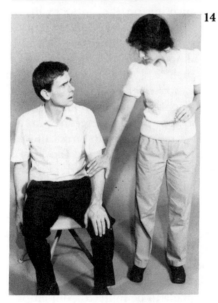

Figures 13 and 14.   In order to smother an impending punch, the clinician enters the Proximal Safety Zone and prevents a clean punch with a "checking block."

Examples of deflecting or blocking are shown in figures 15 through 21. In figure 15, moving from the Nonthreatening Protected Posture, the clinician stays sideways, watches the patient's eyes and keeps the hands high in order to protect the head and throat. In figure 16, the clinician pivots to one side, and blocks the patient's high punch outward rather than directly opposing the patient's force. In figure 17, the clinician brings both forearms downward quickly to protect the abdomen against the patient's midsection attack. In figure 18, the clinician has been unable to avoid the force of the blow and so tucks the chin and clenches the teeth, and absorbs most of the force against the hands and arms rather than directly against the head or throat. In figure 19, the clinician absorbs the force of a low kick against the shin rather than against the groin or abdomen. In figure 20, the clinician who has fallen or been knocked to the ground protects against further attack by continually pivoting on the buttocks in order to keep the feet toward the patient in a position to block. In figure 21, in order to protect against the patient's attack with an object (here, a sharp knife although the response can be the same against a blunt object such as a club or against a thrown object), the clinician utilizes another object (here, a chair, although another common object such as a book, clipboard, jacket, pillow, or mattress may also be appropriate) defensively as a shield: Note that the clinician does not attempt to strike the patient, but rather uses the object as a safe buffer and blocking instrument. Two or more clinicians may utilize a mattress or other similar object to maneuver the patient who is armed (or who has an object with which to harm the self) toward a wall or corner, where the patient can be briefly pinned so as to prevent movement and make possible further restraint and recovery of the dangerous object. In the event that no blocking object is available, then the clinician can employ the same empty-handed deflection and blocking maneuvers as against a punch or kick. While the clinician is likely to be injured from empty-handed defense against a weapon, such a sacrifice may prove necessary in order to survive an attack. Certainly, the clinician should recognize when to call for the assistance of others.

Figure 15. The clinician stands sideways with hands held high in anticipation of attack.

Figure 16. The clinician pivots away from the patient's attack and deflects the punch with the palms.

17

Figure 17.   Alternatively, the clinician pivots and blocks with the forearms.

18

Figure 18.   As a last resort, the clinician pivots and absorbs the blow against the hands and arms rather than against the head or throat.

Figure 19. Against a kick, the clinician absorbs the blow against the shin rather than against the groin or abdomen.

Figure 20. In order to protect the self from the ground, the clinician keeps the feet toward the patient and blocks kicks with the soles.

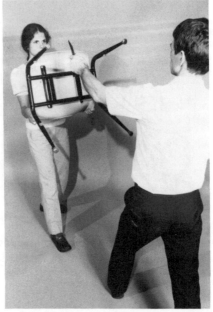

**Figure 21.   Against an attack with a knife, the clinician
defends with an appropriate object as a shield.**

Against Wrist Grabbing and Related Attacks

As in protection against punching, kicking, and similar attacks, prevention is the superior defense against wrist grabbing and related attacks. Certainly, one can avoid being grabbed by staying within the Distal Safety Zone. Alternatively, one can attempt to pivot and deflect the patient's attempted grab as in figures 22 and 23. Such a maneuver is also applicable against an attempted push. Should the patient actually grab the clinician by the wrist, the clinician may elect to allow the patient to maintain the grab while attempting verbal and nonverbal intervention measures (including asking the patient to let go). Such attacks are not typically life threatening. Should the clinician judge the necessity of physically effecting an escape, maneuvers such those depicted in figures 24 through 32 can be implemented. Figures 24 through 29 depict releases which are

Figures 22 and 23. The clinician averts an attempted grab or push by pivoting out of the way and deflecting the patient's arms.

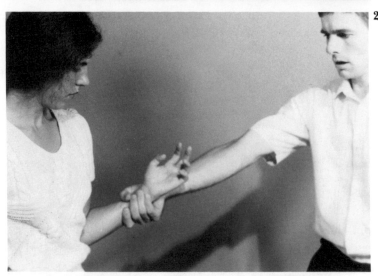

Figures 24, 25, and 26.   The clinician bends the arm at the elbow for added strength and swiftly torques against the patient's thumb to effect the release.

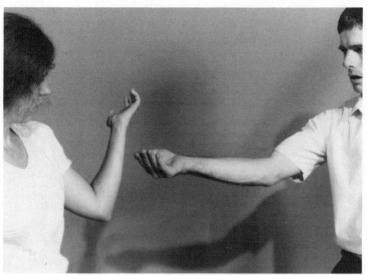

26

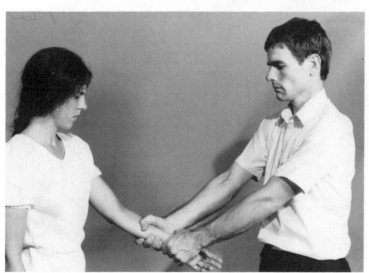

27

Figures 27, 28, and 29.   The clinician reaches in with the free hand and assists the captured hand's release, going against the patient's thumbs.

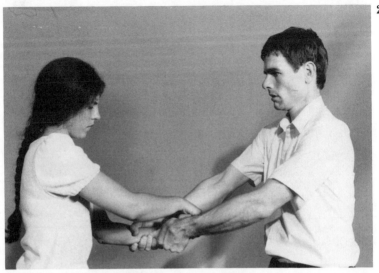

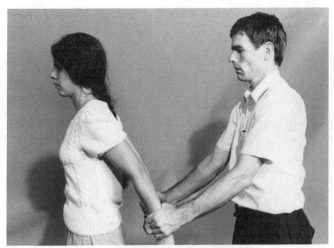

30

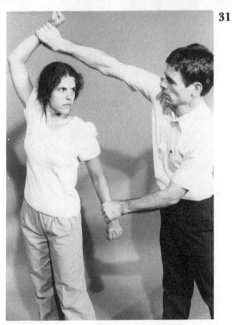

31

Figures 30, 31, and 32.   The clinician bends one arm at
the elbow for added strength,
turns to face the patient, and
escapes when the patient is in an
untenable position.

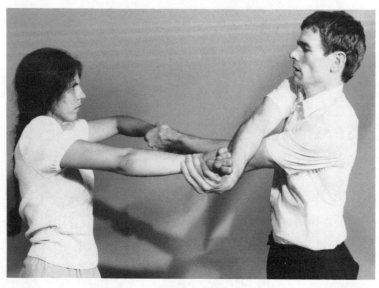

effected by directing the clinician's effort against the patient's thumbs, which are the weakest point of the grip: Note that an attempt to proceed directly against the patient's fingers would be unlikely to work. Figures 30 through 32 depict an escape in which the clinician maneuvers the patient into an untenable position before exiting against the thumbs. In all of these maneuvers, the clinician maximizes strength by bending the arm at the elbow and executes the techniques swiftly, before the patient has time to react to and to further resist the procedure. In actual practice, it may be necessary to actively distract the patient in order to gain the opportunity to precipitously escape.

Against Hair Grabbing and Related Attacks

Grabbing the hair can be quite painful; grabbing lips, ears, and other sensitive areas can additionally lead to serious and permanent injury. Such attacks, and other situations such as scratching, pinching, and grabbing of clothing or dangerous objects may be handled in a similar manner when primary prevention has failed. The first priority in dealing with such attacks is to immediately establish control over the grabbing hand in order to minimize further damage. Once this control has been established, depending upon the particulars of the situation, the clinician may find it possible to reposition the grabbing hand into a mechanically inferior position from which full escape is possible; or it may prove necessary for the clinician either to negotiate with the patient for release or to call upon others for assistance. Such sequences are depicted in figures 33 through 40. In figures 33 through 38, control is established by pulling the patient's grabbing hand firmly down against the head, so that the patient is unable to cause further pain or damage by pulling or shaking. The final point of both sequences is a position in which the patient is at such a mechanical disadvantage that further grabbing is difficult. Note that the clinician must neither induce pain nor lock the patient's wrist joint, but rather maneuver into a point at which the patient's grip is weakened. The clinician is likely to lose some hair in this process. In figures 39 through 40, control is established when the clinician grabs the patient's grabbing hand. Even though it may not be realistically possible to directly reposition the patient's hand into an untenable position, the immediate danger from the hair grab is terminated and negotiation can begin or help can be summoned. Once control has been established, the worst danger is past and an opportunity to distract the patient may develop, or the clinician may actively distract the patient by covering the patient's eyes, etc., for a brief instant in which to escape. In case of other types of grabbing, a similar maneuver may be attempted in which the grabbing hand is captured so that it cannot continue to pull sharply. Figures 41 and 42 demonstrate the recommended procedure for effecting release of a captured body part or object from a firm grip, assuming that control has already been established over the grabbing hand. The thumb is moved into a position directly against the metacarpus. Note that the thumb is not pulled away from the rest of the hand (nor are the fingers pried), but rather is pushed toward the base of the first finger (it may prove necessary to have one or more clinicians work together to maintain control over the grabbing hand while another clinician performs the release maneuver). Once the thumb has been removed from

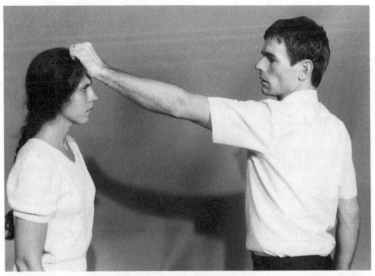

33

34

**Figures 33, 34, and 35.   The clinician first establishes
control over the grabbing hand,
and then repositions it into a
mechanically inferior position.**

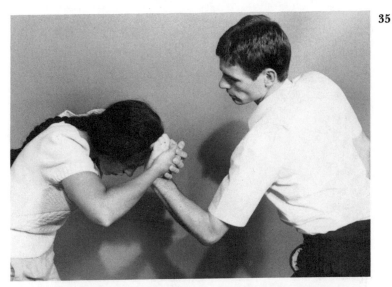

35

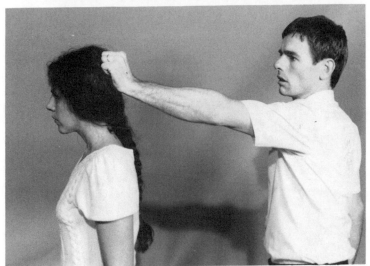

36

Figures 36, 37, and 38.   Again, the clinician first establishes control over the grabbing hand, and then repositions it into a mechanically inferior position.

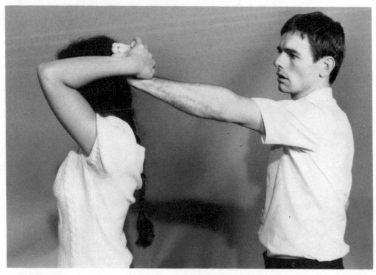

37

38

Figures 39 and 40.   The clinician turns in order to establish control over the grabbing hand.

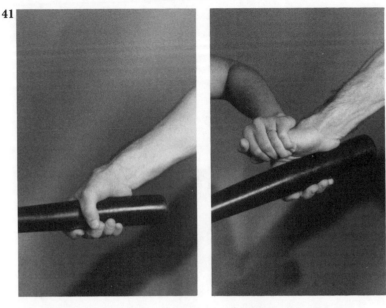

**Figures 41 and 42.   In order to weaken the grip, the clin-
ician moves the thumb of the grab-
bing hand against the metacarpus.**

gripping in this way, the strength of the grip is broken and
escape or removal can be completed (gradually, if necessary,
by wedging a bit at a time and waiting to move until the patient tires).

Against Encirclement

Although encirclement (e.g., "bear hug") is frightening, it
is not typically a direct threat to life. If encirclement has not
been successfully prevented nor interrupted, the clinician must
not panic, but rather can often simply wait, raise the legs from
the floor so that the patient must carry the clinician's entire
weight, and wait for the patient to tire. Due to anaerobic tiring,
the patient will not be able to sustain a full-force grip, and the
clinician will be able to breathe by taking small gulps of air as
the patient tires. The encirclement is actually a weak way to

hold one in the air, and only a rather small amount of slack is needed to allow release. The clinician can gradually wedge a bit at a time by clasping the hands and pulling them upward (forcing the clinician's upper arms outward), turn the head to one side, and at an opportune moment precipitously drop free. Such a sequence is shown in figures 43 through 45.

Against Choking

With good reason, choking is one of the most frightening of all possible attacks, one for which primary prevention must be emphasized. However, when primary prevention fails there still may be an opportunity to interrupt the attack provided that one moves swiftly to protect the throat. Unless the choke is forcefully and expertly applied, the clinician will have several seconds to take action before losing consciousness. A sequence of maneuvers against different types of chokes is shown in figures 46 through 54. The essential aspect of each release consists in the clinician's tucking the chin downward as close to the chest as possible. This maneuver flexes the neck muscles, drives the critical air and blood circulation structures farther from the surface of the neck, and makes it more difficult for the patient to get a solid grip around the neck. In figures 46 through 51, after the throat is protected in this manner, release is effected when the clinician raises one hand and turns, utilizing torque and leverage to remove the patient's hands. Figures 52 through 54 depict the defense against an "arm bar" choke, a very serious situation. The first and essential maneuver is for the clinician to tuck the chin behind the patient's arm while pulling downward with both hands against the patient's arm (using all of the clinician's weight and strength). If this maneuver is successful, then the immediate danger of fatality is past and the clinician may remain in this uncomfortable (though not life threatening) position indefinitely while waiting, negotiating, or calling for help. Direct and immediate escape is not necessary, but the clinician may have an opportunity to gain release from the headlock by pushing (rather than pulling as initially) against the patient's arm and backing out.

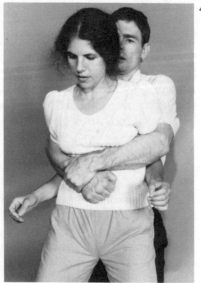

43

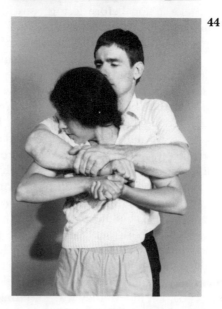
44

Figures 43, 44, and 45. The clinician anaerobically tires
the patient, wedges the patient's
arms bit by bit, and suddenly
drops free.

45

Against Biting

Biting is another attack for which there is no substitute for prevention. However, in the event that the patient is maintaining a prolonged bite the clinician can minimize tissue damage by avoiding the impulse to jerk the bitten part free, and the natural impulse to strike or otherwise inflict pain upon the biting patient. Jerking the bitten part may result in further tearing, and inflicting pain may cause the patient to bite even harder. Instead, the clinician must push the bitten part even deeper into the patient's mouth; sometimes this maneuver will by itself create a brief opportunity for escape because it is unexpected and uncomfortable for the patient. The clinician may also hold the patient's nostrils closed as depicted in figure 55. The patient typically takes in a brief gasp of air in response

46

47

48

Figures 46, 47, and 48. The clinician first tucks the chin,
then raises one hand and turns,
using torque and leverage.

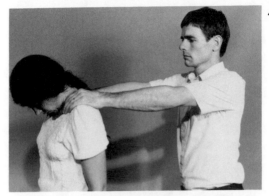

Figures 49, 50, and 51. Again, the clinician first tucks the chin, then raises one hand and turns, using torque and leverage.

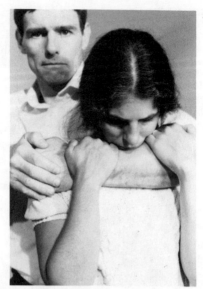

52

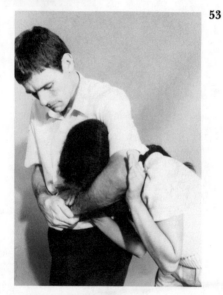

53

Figures 52, 53, and 54.   The clinician tucks the chin behind the patient's arm while pulling downward with both hands; if possible, the clinician then exits the headlock.

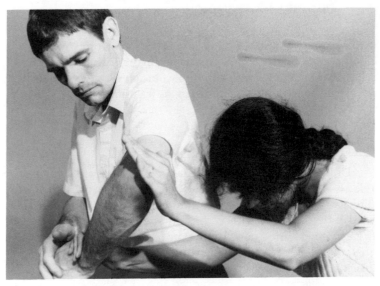

54

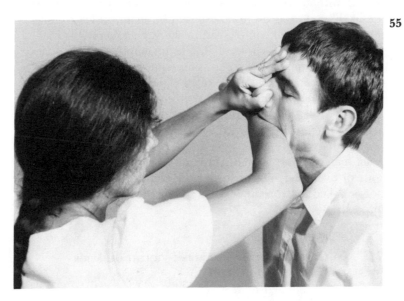

55

Figure 55.   Against a bite, the clinician distracts the pa-
            tient by pushing the bitten part deeper into
            the patient's mouth, closing the patient's
            nostrils, and covering the patient's eyes.

to this maneuver and the clinician has an opportunity to escape. Finally, sometimes the patient can be further distracted by covering the patient's eyes with the clinician's fingers, a towel, etc. Teamwork by several clinicians is a definite asset in such a situation.

Against Firearm

Unlike defenses against other types of attack, it is reasonable to address only the *threat* of use of a firearm against the clinician rather than its actual use. The clinician who is threatened by the patient with a firearm should recognize that the firearm almost invariably is an expression of feelings of inadequacy and fear. Therefore the clinician should attempt to speak directly to the underlying psychological issue. The clinician may be somewhat relieved to recognize that if a short time can be passed without the patient's actually discharging the firearm, the likelihood of its eventual use is quite small. At least initially, the clinician should comply with whatever demands the patient may make, and the clinician should take special care to avoid upsetting the patient further. The clinician must not attempt to talk the patient into handing the firearm over to the clinician, but rather should suggest that the patient point the weapon away while they talk, and at an appropriate time might suggest that the patient place the weapon in a safe, neutral place (rather than handing the weapon over, because the patient may react fearfully, impulsively, or clumsily at the instant of passing control over the firearm to the clinician). The patient should not be asked to drop the firearm because it may discharge upon impact.

OTHER ASPECTS OF MANAGING VIOLENT BEHAVIOR

Safe Environment and Attire

No environment which is sufficiently enriched to be truly therapeutic can ever be completely devoid of hazardous design features and objects; however, preventive attention can minimize possible hazards and at the very least prevent the clinician being taken by surprise. In some appropriate settings, massive rubberized furniture (too heavy and bulky to throw) is utilized, along with light nonglass ashtrays, paper medicine and drinking cups, and emergency "personal distress devices" (cf. Doms, 1984). Whenever possible, a large interview room should be available for interviewing potentially violent patients, with at least two exits (doorless is ideal) and the possibility of placing a desk between patient and clinician.

The clinician's own clothing should be appropriate to the demands of the workplace: Attire should be functional, non-provocative, and consistent with the professional image of the clinician. Adequate footwear is an often overlooked aspect. Should the clinician have even a brief opportunity to prepare for physical intervention (for instance, before a group intervention for the purpose of secluding a spiraling patient) the clinician should take the opportunity to make attire as safe as possible to the self, other clinicians, and the patient by removing watch, pen, badge, belt buckle, jewelry, earrings, necktie, scarf, hearing aid and glasses (if possible), and by tying long hair back out of the way and rolling up shirtsleeves.

Hostage Situations

Hostage-taking situations in various mental health settings have been described by Qadir (1982) and by Turner (1984a, 1984b); a written organizational response plan for dealing with such incidents is highly recommended in order to avert shock and confusion (cf. Taitz, 1984; Turner, 1985). A professional police hostage negotiator must be brought into the situation as soon as possible; until that professional arrives, any clinician interacting with the hostage taker should attempt to keep the person talking, if possible, without agreeing to meet any specific demands (cf. Turner, 1984a, 1984b). The clinician who is taken hostage should recognize that the first few minutes of the incident are typically the most dangerous of all, and at that time the hostage taker is likely to be even more emotionally upset than the hostage (cf. Fuqua & Wilson, 1978; Turner, 1984a, 1984b). During this initial period the clinician should (a) do

exactly as the hostage taker says, (b) refrain from speaking unless spoken to, (c) avoid an open display of despair, and (d)
remain observant. Following this first stage of the crisis, the
clinician should allow rapport to develop on the hostage taker's
own terms (avoiding cloying pseudoempathy and authoritarian
pseudoprofessionalism). Hostage takers are known to have difficulty in killing hostages with whom they have become person-
ally acquainted during an incident (cf. Aston, 1980; Fuqua &
Wilson, 1978; Pizer, 1980; Turner, 1984a); therefore the clinician should accept any favors or interaction offered, and should
never argue with the hostage taker. If a suicidal or homicidal
theme begins to develop in the hostage taker's conversation, the
clinician should attempt to guide the conversation onto a different topic (Turner, 1984a). The clinician should refrain from
attempting to escape or overpower the hostage taker unless absolutely certain of success. In the event of a rescue attempt,
the clinician should expect explosions, noise, and confusion,
and should lie on the floor until the situation is resolved (Turner, 1984a). Finally, following such an incident, a debriefing
involving both involved and noninvolved clinicians and patients
will be an emotional necessity (cf. Aston, 1980; Taitz, 1984;
Turner, 1984a).

Bomb Threats

Telephoned bomb threats are another unfortunate fact of
professional life (cf. Fuqua & Wilson, 1978; Taitz, 1984; Turner,1985). As with hostage-taking incidents, a written organizational response plan is a worthwhile precaution. The condition
of patients in many mental health facilities may preclude routine evacuation as a precautionary measure in the event of a
bomb threat, unless there is a compelling reason to believe that
a threat is genuine (cf. Taitz, 1984). Among the indicators believed to be associated with genuine threats are specifically
stated motivation, time and place for the explosion (especially
after hours, weekends), and longer, detailed calls (Taitz, 1984).

Chapter 9

EMERGENCY PATIENT CONTROL

Seclusion, Restraint, and Medication

At times the patient's behavior must be controlled through physical methods. The most common of these physical methods are seclusion, restraint, and medication. Seclusion consists in placing the patient into a controlled environment where the patient cannot harm others and in which environmental (including interpersonal) stimulation is reduced to a minimum. Manual restraint consists in physically holding the patient for the purpose of control and/or transportation. Mechanical restraint consists in applying devices (such as limb restraints and straitjackets) which limit or prevent some or all of the patient's movements. Medication involves the oral or parenteral administration of substances which affect the patient's physical and psychological processes. Emergency seclusion, restraint, and medication are legitimate crisis intervention procedures; at times they are absolutely essential for proper care and treatment of the patient. Even agencies and institutions with explicit policies against nonemergency use of such techniques must recognize the occasional necessity of their temporary emergency use to prevent harm to the patient, others, or to the therapeutic environment and milieu. The present discussion will be restricted to the applications of seclusion, mechanical restraint, and medication to the management of violent crisis situations: Other nonemergency applications are expertly discussed elsewhere (e.g., Barry, 1984; Gast & Nelson, 1977; Gutheil, 1978; Liberman, Marshall & Burke, 1981; Lion, 1975a, 1983a; Plutchik, Karasu, Conte, Siegel & Jerrett, 1978; Sheard, 1984; Soloff, 1983; Tardiff, 1984b).

Like other therapeutic measures, seclusion, restraint, and medication have purposes, indications, contraindications, and possible complications. No single measure is necessarily the treatment of choice for aggression; rather, the preferred intervention depends upon the etiology of the instance of aggressive behavior under consideration and other relevant aspects of the patient and the situation. One or more of these emergency control measures may be inappropriate for the individual patient (e.g., some patients' physiological condition may contraindicate medication or restraint), or some combination of measures may be appropriate (e.g., medication and seclusion may be preferable to restraint for some patients). Although the clinician's treatment philosophy will necessarily affect the timing and frequency with which particular emergency control measures are implemented (Okin, 1985; Soloff, 1983, in press; Soloff, Gutheil & Wexler, 1985), mere convenience to the clinician or punitive value are never part of a legitimate rationale (Dix, in press; Ennis & Siegel, 1973; Soloff, 1983; Woody & Associates, 1984).

Often, in emergency situations, the patient is unwilling to undergo some or all of these procedures, and the clinician must always be mindful to offer the least restrictive alternative. However, as previously discussed, there is no consensus as to the relative restrictiveness of seclusion, mechanical restraint, and medication. Furthermore, in an emergency the clinician has the clear responsibility to take action to protect the patient and others from harm, even when such protection entails implementation of procedures against the patient's will. As in other instances, *judgment* is the central mechanism available to the clinician for determination of the course of action which is best defended on clinical and on legal grounds. Although an actual episode of aggressive patient behavior directed against other persons is the most clear-cut and obvious indication for the use of involuntary control procedures, the clinician need not defer vigorous intervention until an actual assault has transpired. Preventive measures are fully justified when the clinician judges them necessary to avert an impending episode of behavior which may be destructive to the self, to other persons, or to the therapeutic environment and milieu (cf. Gutheil, 1978, 1980; Gutheil & Tardiff, 1984; Soloff, 1983; Soloff, Gutheil & Wexler, 1985). Furthermore, although the clinician must first *consider* less restrictive methods for managing aggressive behavior (for instance, verbal and nonverbal communication), such methods need not necessarily be *attempted* first when they are unlikely to be of benefit and a delay may prove detrimental to the patient and/or others. Clinically, the decision to intervene is more often made too late rather than too early, and such an error is characteristic of the neophyte rather than the seasoned clinician (cf. Ellman, 1985). Frequently, *offering* seclusion, restraint, medication, or discharge will be welcomed by the patient if done before the patient has completely lost control.

TEAMWORK

Communication

Teamwork is essential to integrate and to synergize the individual efforts of clinicians. Adequate organizational leadership and a warm, facilitative interpersonal environment can enhance the effectiveness of the individual clinician; some kinds of psychological and physical interventions can only occur when several clinicians work smoothly in concert.

Interclinician communication is the most difficult task in a crisis situation—a task perhaps even more difficult than direct negotiation with the aggressive patient—and violent emergencies produce special patterns of clinician stress and communication dysfunction (cf. Cornfield & Fielding, 1980; Nickens, 1984). In such a situation, both a clinical leader and a clinical task must be agreed upon. Leadership can be determined by both formal criteria (most senior staff, patient's primary therapist) and by situational criteria (the clinician who is least threatening to a fearful patient or who feels most confident with particular procedure). Specific training and practice with simulation exercises can help all clinicians reach a consensual understanding of treatment philosophy and acceptable approaches within a given clinical setting: Adequately trained groups of clinicians who come to know one another well can form stable, valid expectations which enable rapid, subtle interclinician communication. Certainly in a crisis situation, once a leader has been agreed upon, directives must be obeyed and disagreements deferred until after the immediate situation has been resolved. Although most clinicians are able and willing to assist one another with physical aspects of patient management, some clinicians have valid reservations (personal, physical, or medical) which preclude their direct involvement in such tasks. There is a useful place for such clinicians during a violent emergency (someone is needed to make telephone calls, prepare medications, ready restraining devices, evacuate other patients, secure the environment, etc.). However, in fairness to the other clinicians, such facts should be made known in advance so that appropriate arrangements and expectations can be agreed upon.

Violence Precautions

Violence precautions are a necessary aspect of teamwork, serving to alert all clinicians to potential hazards and to help clinicians avoid unknowing precipitation of an untoward event (Hart, Broad & Trimborn, 1984; Kalogerakis, 1971; Nickens, 1984). Although one must be concerned with the effects of "labeling" the patient (and perhaps creating a self-fulfilling prophecy), the potential risk is too great to dispense with such measures. Although specific procedures will vary as a function of clinical setting, all staff—both clinical and nonclinical—must be sensitized to the need to alert others to suspected violence potential (receptionists, security officers, housekeeping personnel are often able to note the patient's agitation before the patient sees the clinician). To be noted, in addition to obvious behavioral signs, are patients with a previous history of violence or threats within the clinical setting, patients brought involuntarily by the police, and patients with a history of violence (outside the clinical setting) in the days before admission. Referring clinicians should certainly alert others of any violence potential in referred patients. Appropriate measures for patients placed on violence precautions include frequent observation with regular charting, explicit discussion regarding proscriptions against violent behavior, searching of patient (and patient's room on inpatient unit), exclusion of provocative relatives or other visitors, and clinician willingness to implement strong preventive measures before impending violence becomes an actuality (cf. Hart, Broad & Trimborn, 1984).

Incident Review

A formal incident review should be conducted following each and every instance of actual or narrowly averted physical intervention (actual or threatened patient assault, restraint, or involuntary seclusion or medication). Both technical and affective issues need to be addressed for clinicians (cf. Di Bella, 1979; Tardiff, 1984) so that the feedback necessary for learning can be given (what worked well, what did not) and that feelings aroused by the intervention can be adequately integrated. Besides the patient actually involved in the incident, other patients will also need factual information and emotional support in order to avert negative effects from the experience.

SECLUSION

The patient's need for decreased stimulation in a secure environment is the primary indication for the choice of seclusion over other emergency control techniques (cf. Gutheil & Tardiff, 1984). Seclusion may also be preferred for other reasons. Medication may not be immediately effective for some conditions (such as manic or catatonic excitement), or may be contraindicated (as when the patient has ingested unknown kinds of other drugs or has otherwise presented a diagnostic puzzle); mechanical restraint may exacerbate the psychological distress of some patients, or may be medically contraindicated (as for hyperthermic or hypertensive patients). Although seclusion has clear benefits for appropriately selected patients, complications of this method of intervention have also been documented. Seclusion is contraindicated for patients whose dysfunctional behavior is presumed to result from excessive isolation and for whom increased rather than decreased stimulation is appropriate. Some patients may become increasingly agitated by seclusion (Mattson & Sacks, 1978) and may experience an exacerbation of hallucinations (Wadeson & Carpenter, 1976) and of unpleasant affects (Plutchik, Karasu, Conte, Siegel & Jerrett, 1978). Seclusion is also contraindicated for patients who may be able to inflict self-harm even when under direct observation (e.g., head banging, self-biting or eye gouging). Patients who witness the seclusion of other patients may misunderstand the purpose and effects of seclusion, and feel angry toward the clinician and fearful for the well-being of themselves and the other patients (cf. Plutchik, Karasu, Conte, Siegel & Jerrett, 1978). Gutheil (1978) has even noted the phenomenon of "seclusion envy" among some patients who see such an intervention as an indication of clinician concern and caring. Although the secluded patient is quite needful of intensive care, Mattson and Sacks (1978) have noted the tendency of the clinician to decrease involvement with the patient following seclusion.

Ideal Physical Characteristics of the Seclusion Room

The physical characteristics of the seclusion room should be supportive of the purposes of seclusion: safety and decreased stimulation. A superlative description of the seclusion room can be found in Samuels and Moriarty (1979b). Among the necessary features:

(1) An extra-wide doorway, with a heavy door which opens outward (so that patients cannot barricade themselves nor trap clinicians inside) with no protruding inside handle. The door should have a strong "throw-bolt" for rapid locking as well as a keyed lock (to prevent unauthorized entry), and an unbreakable observation window.

(2) Smooth, strong walls and flooring without moldings or

protuberances of any kind (carpet, tile, and padding are unsafe) with heating/cooling vents mounted out of reach on walls or ceiling and covered by secure screening. Although scientific evidence for the effectiveness of the "tranquilizing pink" hypothesis is scant at best (cf. Pellegrini, Schauss, & Miller, 1981), a subdued color of nontoxic paint seems reasonable. Windows should be shatterproof, without ledges, and covered by secure screening.

(3) A ceiling that is unreachable, with recessed, externally controlled (rheostat preferable) light fixtures covered by secure screening.

(4) An uncovered foam mattress. If a bed frame is to be used, it should be specially constructed for strength, safety, and accommodation of mechanical restraining devices when necessary: It should also be bolted to the floor (cf. Hay & Cromwell, 1980).

(5) The room must be large enough for physical accommodation of the patient and five clinicians. There must be no other objects in the room.

Seclusion Procedures

Even though seclusion may be an emergency procedure, for the reassurance of the patient it is incumbent upon the clinician to handle the situation professionally and with as much an air of the "routine" as possible (cf. Tardiff, 1984b); of course, such an attitude should not lead to a casual attitude toward the ordering of seclusion, which should remain a special intensive care procedure. The most senior clinician available should make the decision to seclude the patient, or should delegate this authority responsibly to another person who will serve as the "leader" during the intervention (because of familiarity with the patient or with the procedure). A physician's order for seclusion should be obtained as soon as possible, although immediately required seclusion should not be delayed, since an order can appropriately be obtained after the fact. Because the act of secluding is itself a communication, the clinician must remain especially sensitive to meaningful aspects of the physical intervention; humiliation of the patient is certainly to be avoided. The following points should be observed (cf. Kronberg, 1983; Lion & Soloff, 1984):

1. Other persons (patients, relatives, visitors) should be removed from the immediate vicinity (to rooms, cafeteria, recreation area) since they may feel the need to protect the secluded patient from the clinicians. It may be appropriate to explain the procedure and its rationale to these other persons.

2. Sufficient numbers of clinicians should be present to ensure that physical control can definitely be effected without undue struggle or danger. Such numbers should be utilized to convey reassuring firmness rather than challenge or threat. Sometimes "underwhelming force" can be effective by decreasing the threat to the patient, although backup must be instantly available. Alternatively, should force be necessary, it should be backed with sufficient personnel so that it is obvious to the patient that struggle is futile. The patient will offer the most vigorous resistance only when there is some perceived possibility that the struggle may actually prove successful. Used properly, a show of force can usually obviate its actual application; however, this must be marshalled before the situation has deteriorated to the point at which the patient has already begun violent resistance. One clinician should be responsible for closing and locking the seclusion room door, and another clinician not involved in the seclusion procedure should serve as "monitor," keeping at a distance to observe and to take notes, and to summon additional aid if necessary. The intervention team should agree (beforehand, if possible) as to leadership authority, options to be considered, physical techniques to be attempted, etc. Training can make such understandings relatively easy to reach, and even in an emergency situation there is sometimes an opportunity to meet for a few seconds of discussion before the intervention.

3. The intervention leader should take the initiative in communicating with the patient. Only rarely will the decision of whether to seclude the patient be made during the actual interaction with the patient (this decision is typically already firm); in contrast, the decision of whether it will be necessary to physically compel the patient to go to the seclusion room

may need to be made by the intervention leader during the interaction with the patient. The rest of the intervention team is not to countermand this decision, but rather should discuss any reservations before or after the encounter with the patient. When appropriate, the reason for seclusion may be briefly explained and the patient given a short period of time to go voluntarily to the seclusion room. If the patient does not go voluntarily, the leader should not hesitate to order immediate physical intervention (a specific code to begin the restraint should be agreed upon beforehand, such as, "restrain now"), and restraining techniques appropriate to the patient and situation should be utilized. It may prove necessary to mechanically restrain or medicate the patient before transportation to the seclusion room.

4. The patient should be searched (typically by a same-gender clinician, except perhaps in case of aggression secondary to homosexual panic), and the patient's shoes, belt, jewelry, and other objects removed; judgment will dictate whether allowing the patient to retain glasses, hearing aid, etc., is a relatively greater danger for self-harm or for increasing disorientation due to sensory distortion. In some settings, placing the patient into pajamas or a gown is appropriate.

5. If the patient is willing, the patient should be instructed to sit next to the wall farthest from the seclusion room exit while the clinicians back is out of the doorway. If the patient is unwilling, assaultive, or attempting to escape, then the patient should be manually restrained in the corner farthest from the exit. Facing the patient away from the doorway and will make it difficult for the patient to see the doorway and the clinicians as they exit. Clinicians should leave one at a time, coordinated by a prearranged signal. The most hazardous point of the procedure is the closing of the door, which must be rapid enough to prevent the patient from leaving but which must be done carefully to prevent injury to patient and clinicians.

6. When emergency seclusion has been initiated by a non-physician, the patient must be *continuously* observed (and physical/mental status documented every 15 minutes) until a physician's order for seclusion (and for less intensive observation) has been obtained and/or the patient has been examined by a physi-

cian (cf. Tardiff, 1984, for relevant guidelines for observation and patient care following emergency seclusion). Special attention must be paid to the patient's mental and physical status; fluid, food, and toileting needs; and cleanliness and comfort. When continuous observation is no longer required, the seclusion room door must be kept locked to prevent unauthorized persons from entering and taking advantage of the secluded patient, bringing contraband, etc.

7. A systematic plan for the patient's eventual release from seclusion is equally important to the plan for initiating seclusion, and should be included as a part of the first consideration of seclusion for the patient. Simply put, seclusion should be ended if the patient becomes significantly better or significantly worse (Fitzgerald & Long, 1973). Certainly, improvement is an indication for the termination of seclusion, but deterioration is also a strong indication that a different course of treatment is indicated (e.g., release from seclusion, mechanical restraint, medication, etc.). Among the signs to be monitored for improvement are potential for harming self and/or others (both threatened and attempted); intensity of fear, anger, anxiety, and agitation; stabilization of mood; adequacy of reality-testing and judgment; degree of perceptual distortion, hallucination, delusion, and other psychotic symptoms; normalization of vital signs (pulse, respiration, blood pressure); regularization of eating, sleeping, and self-care functions; and ability to cooperate and interact appropriately. It is best to "wean" the patient from seclusion gradually, perhaps by proceeding from working with the patient in locked seclusion, to unlocked seclusion with door open, to a relatively isolated regular private room (Baradell, 1985). The patient's ability to maintain behavioral control at each progressive step is closely monitored. Should the patient be unable to function in the less secure and less stimulating settings, a return to previously acceptable environmental conditions may be indicated. The clinician's first attempt at reentry to the seclusion room (for example, for toileting of the patient or other care) is critical and perhaps the most dangerous (cf. Lion, Snyder & Merrill, 1981). The seclusion room should never be entered without adequate backup personnel; however, the clinician must judge whether to enter seclusion alone in order

to decrease apparent threat or to be accompanied by several others for a "show of force." If the patient is able to communicate verbally, the clinician should make a specific behavioral request of the patient (such as, "sit on the floor against the wall") both for physical safety and to assess the patient's ability and intention to cooperate. The verbal patient should also be told specifically what behavior is required for gaining release from seclusion (sit quietly and talk with the clinician for 30 minutes; take medications; desist from threats and attempts to harm others). Whether interacting with verbal or with nonverbal patients, upon entering the seclusion room the clinician should at first stand in a sideways posture next to the wall beside the door: This position leaves the clinician with quick access to egress, yet does not "crowd" (standing against the wall allows maximum distance between clinician and patient) the patient nor block the patient's view of the exit. Finally, the rest of the patient milieu must be sufficiently settled before releasing the secluded patient (cf. Soloff, 1983).

8. A review and processing of each and every episode of seclusion is absolutely essential for the secluded patient, for other patients, and for the clinician. The patient will need special attention and help to make use of the seclusion experience without being overwhelmed by fear, anger, or guilt, and to explore alternatives to the behaviors that led to seclusion. Other patients will need explanation and reassurance. The clinicians should give and receive feedback, both of a technical nature regarding decision making and the implementation of seclusion, and of an affective/interpersonal nature regarding feelings and perceptions that occurred during the process.

RESTRAINT

Manual Restraint

At times it is necessary to manually restrain the patient and/or to transport the patient from place to place. Due to struggle and constant adaptation to the patient's resistance strategies, with manual restraint and transportation procedures (perhaps more so than with other maneuvers) the clinician will find that positions depicted here will be prototypical goals rather than actualities. However, such prototypical goals give the clinician an idea about what kinds of positions to attempt to produce. When improvising, the clinician must be especially careful not to bend the patient's joints in the wrong direction, not to induce pain, not to knock down or drop the patient, and not to inadvertently strangle the patient nor to compromise the patient's ability to breathe (when restraining the patient on a bed or rug, or through inadvertent pressure upon the patient's throat, thorax, or abdomen). The clinician should also recall that haptic communication is one of the last functions lost by the disturbed patient. Even though the patient may be otherwise unable to communicate, the patient will probably be able to "read" the quality of touch during restraint and transportation. Except in an absolute emergency, such procedures should not be attempted by a single clinician, but rather by a team of several clinicians. However, in exceptional circumstances, the clinician may judge the necessity of immediate solo intervention. Figures 56 through 58 illustrate prototypical methods for solo manual restraint: The individual clinician, patient, and situation will determine which method is preferable or indeed possible. For all three methods, the clinician must have physical strength at least approximately equal to that of the patient. In each case, the clinician ideally attempts to approach the patient from behind and maintain close chest-to-back contact with the patient, staying out of the Danger Zone, and the clinician must beware of a possible head-bash, bite, foot-stomp, or similar attack by the patient. For the latter two restraining methods, the clinician will typically begin with the "bear hug" restraint and maneuver from that position into a different restraining technique if appropriate.

In the event that one or more clinicians must attempt to separate two patients who are involved in an altercation with one another, the patient should be approached from behind as shown in figure 59 and grasped over rather than under the arms. The clinician must remember never to get in between two fighting patients, and solo intervention is especially risky in such a situation. It may prove easier to turn the patients

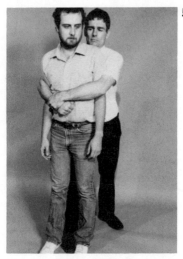

Figure 56. "Bear hug" solo manual restraining maneuver. The patient is grasped from behind, over the elbow joints.

Figure 57. Variant of solo manual restraining technique. One of the patient's arms is grasped from behind and held against the patient; pressure is maintained over the elbow joint.

Figure 58. "Wrap-up" variant of solo manual restraining technique. Both arms are grasped from behind and drawn downward and across the patient's torso.

away from one another rather than to pull them backward. There are several psychological aspects to intervening in a fight. It may be possible to order one of the combatants to leave, or to distract one or both (grabbing a patient from behind even without intention of maintaining control may be one way to effect such a distraction). The clinician may consider restraining the weaker patient and turning that patient away from the other patient (regardless of which patient is the apparent aggressor) in order to be more sure of being physically able to terminate the altercation.

When more than one clinician is available, more effective manual restraint and patient transportation procedures can be implemented. Figures 60 and 61 show underarm supportive positions. The patient's weight is supported axially against the crook of the clinician's arm (rather than by the clinician's hands).

59

Figure 59.   In order to separate two fighting patients, the clinician approaches from behind.

Such positions maximize the clinician's strength and are comfortable and quite safe for both the patient and the clinician. The underarm supportive position is an excellent method for lifting or lowering the patient, as shown in figure 62. When lifting, the clinicians should keep their backs as perpendicular to the ground as possible and lift with the thigh muscles. For the safety of both patient and clinician, with any transportation technique, the clinician must be certain not to attempt to move the patient until restraining control has been established over the patient (one may have to tire the patient by prolonged manual [or even mechanical] restraint or may need to medicate the patient in order to gain sufficient control to attempt transportation); likewise the patient must be set back down and restraint

Figure 60.   Underarm supportive manual restraint and
transportation position.

Figure 61.   Alternate underarm supportive manual
restraint and transportation position. In this
position, because the patient's arm is straightened, it is relatively weaker.

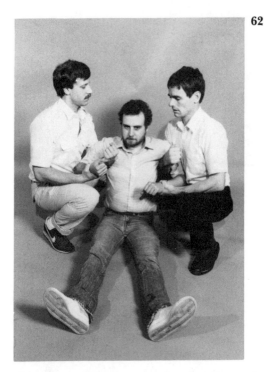

**Figure 62.   The underarm supportive position can be
used to lift or to lower the patient.**

reestablished if during transportation the control over the patient should become unreliable. For a minimally resistive (un-
steady or confused) patient, the underarm supportive position
can be utilized by a single clinician to help a patient walk, or
go up and down stairs.

For patients who offer more vigorous resistance, the underarm supportive position can be utilized to walk the patient
backwards, as shown in figure 63. The patient is less able to
resist when being taken backwards, and also cannot see the optimal places at which to increase resistance (such as doorways).
By keeping the patient's arms across the clinicians' chests, the
patient's arm is relatively weaker than if the patient were able
to crook the elbow. As shown in figures 64 and 65, from both

63

Figure 63.   The supportive position can be utilized to walk a resistive patient backwards.

the forward and backwards underarm supportive position, if necessary, other clinicians can assist in carrying the patient by lifting the patient at the knee joints in the crooks of their arms.

An alternative restraining and transportation method for the resistant patient consists in the two-person wrap-up technique, as demonstrated in figure 66. The wrap-up position can also be utilized to manually restrain the patient in a supine position or in a prone position, as demonstrated in figures 67 and 68, respectively. In general, this wrap-up position is effective in holding the patient down (e.g., into a chair or onto a litter); however, the wrap-up is less effective for holding the patient up off the floor (in which case the underarm supportive position is preferable).

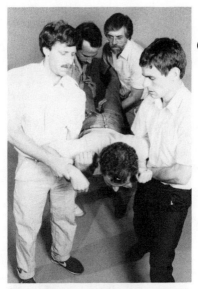

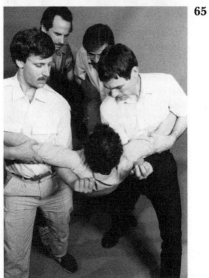

Figures 64 and 65. Other clinicians can assist in carrying the patient from both the forward and backwards supportive position by supporting the patient's legs in the crooks of their arms.

Figure 66.   Two-person wrap-up technique for restraint
and transportation.

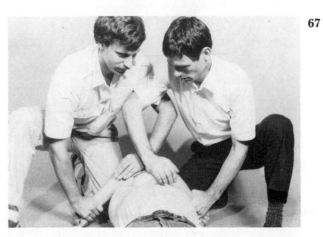

Figures 67 and 68.   Utilizing the wrap-up position for
supine and for prone manual re-
straint, respectively.

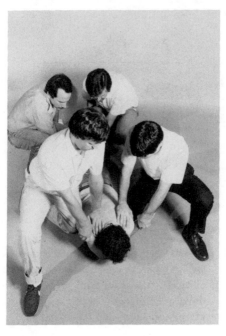

As shown in figures 69 and 70, the patient can also be restrained with the arms straightened to decrease their strength. The clinicians use their body weight (to augment muscular strength) to press directly down against major joints (for safety and leverage). Limbs need not be held static against the floor; instead, the clinician can maintain effective control by guiding the patient's limbs away at an angle to the direction of the patient's intended movements. The patient's attention will be divided among the various limbs that are being restrained, thus hindering escape efforts. The clinician must also utilize proper technique for capturing the patient's legs as shown in figure 71. First, the clinician must approach from the patient's midsection, rather than from below the patient's feet, to avoid being kicked. Second, the clinician must not attempt to reach for the patient's leg with a straightforward grab (palms facing one another, thumbs inward to grasp the leg) because the patient could kick sharply and injure the clinician's thumbs, likely breaking through the attempted grab to strike the clinician's body. Instead, the clinician should cross the arms and make

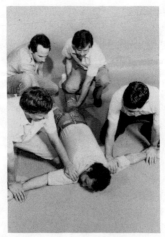

Figure 69.   The patient can be restrained prone with arms
straightened to decrease their strength. All
clinicians use their body weight to press
downward directly over a major joint for
safety and increased leverage.

Figure 70.   The patient can also be restrained supine by
the same general method. Note the clinician
holding the patient under the jaw and pressing down against the forehead to prevent
biting.

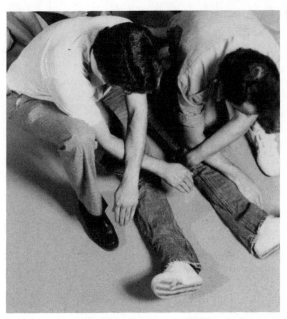

Figure 71. Two clinicians demonstrate proper technique for capturing the patient's legs, by approaching from the patient's midsection rather than from below feet, and by keeping arms crossed in a checking block until contact with the knee is made.

contact with the backs of the hands and forearms in a checking block (thus protecting the thumbs, and also preventing the patient's kick from breaking through the block). After firm contact against the patient's leg has been made, the clinician can slide the hands into the preferred palm-downward restraining position over a major joint.

Mechanical Restraint

Mechanical restraints must be utilized when clinicians are unable to manually restrain the patient and when other measures (such as seclusion) are contraindicated. For the most part, both the emergency and the nonemergency procedures for implementing mechanical restraint are analogous to procedures for implementing seclusion (cf. Tardiff, 1984b), and as with seclusion, once the decision to mechanically restrain the patient has been made, it may be possible to persuade the patient to cooperate voluntarily with the procedure (Nickens, 1984). Mechanical restraint may be the intervention of choice when it is not possible to manually restrain the patient due to the strength of the patient or duration of the restraint (or when the patient cannot be safely transported otherwise), when patient's aggressive or dangerous behavior is due to an unknown etiology, or when the patient's physical condition contraindicates medication. Mechanical restraint can actually be a positive influence upon interpersonal processing with the patient. As Telintelo, Kuhlman and Winget (1983) have noted, because patients and clinicians alike typically fear patient aggression, with restraint the patients'

> preoccupying burden has been taken from them, and they are, ironically, freer to devote attention to exploring the meaning and amelioration of their problems. The restraining therapist, in turn, need no longer be vigilant to signs of impending danger and thus is freer to listen to and attempt to understand the patient (p. 165).

Although mechanical restraint is a technology for which there is no adequate substitute when utilized appropriately, it is easily misused. Mechanical restraint must be instituted in response to the *patient's* needs rather than in response to the clinician's fears or lack of appropriate resources. As Rosen and DiGiacomo (1978) have stated: "It must be strongly emphasized that the decision to place a patient in restraints is an indication for increased rather than decreased observation and care" (p. 229). It is also noteworthy that some retarded patients have been found to enjoy mechanical restraint, and even attempt to place themselves into restraining devices (Favell, McGimsey & Jones, 1978; Favell, McGimsey, Jones & Cannon, 1981).

The restrained patient is at risk for asphyxiation, strangulation, ischemia, muscle cramping, decubiti, hyperthermia, dehydration, and (upon release from restraint) orthostatic hypotension. Therefore close observation is essential, especially in initial stages of restraint before a physician has examined the patient (when observation and the clinician's presence must be continuous, with vital signs recorded every 5 minutes). The restrained patient must be periodically fed, given fluids, toileted (with bedpan if necessary), and bathed. Special care must be taken to ensure the patient's comfort insofar as possible. Properly instituted, mechanical restraint should not cause undue discomfort, pain, or injury. Restrained limbs must be released (one at a time) at least hourly and gently rotated throughout their range of motion. Certainly, however, sufficient staff must be on hand for this procedure. Massage and repositioning should be performed frequently. Because restraint often allows more interpersonal contact between patient and clinician than does seclusion, verbal and nonverbal communications and orientation should be attempted frequently.

Although various other types of restraining apparatus are being developed (cf. Lion & Soloff, 1984), at this writing two commonly used devices are (a) the camisole, with sleeves that tie in the back, maintaining the patient's arms in a crossed position over the chest, and (b) four-point restraints (one for each wrist and ankle) used to tie the patient onto a bed. Practice beforehand is essential to the proper and efficient application of all restraining devices. Inappropriately applied, restraining devices are likely either to allow the patient to escape or to lead to patient injury or death (especially by strangulation).

Camisoles can be color-coded for rapid selection of proper size; some kinds are most easily applied when turned inside out first (so that the patient's arms can more readily be fully inserted into the length of the camisole sleeve, simultaneously turning the camisole right side out). In order to apply the camisole efficiently, the clinician should have sufficient numbers of assistants, and rather than rushing and attempting to apply the camisole all at once, should instead concentrate on accomplishing one substep at a time (first one sleeve, then the other). The patient who is mechanically restrained in a camisole may still be allowed to walk about (typically in a seclusion room, especially in an emergency) if clinically indicated. The camisole may also allow the patient to be transported via wheelchair.

Four-point restraints should ideally be applied with a bed specifically designed for use with these devices (cf. Hay & Cromwell, 1980). When such a special bed is unavailable (or when the patient is being restrained to a litter for transportation), the bed rails should be kept lowered and the restraints tied to the bed frame (away from the patient's reach) rather than to the side rails (so that if they are inadvertently lowered at a later time they will not pull on the restraints and possibly injure the patient); the bed should be flat and lowered to its lowest position, and the wheels locked. Ankle and wrist restraints should be padded, and must not cinch tightly when the patient moves against them; many modern types are specifically designed to prevent this complication. Restraints are sufficiently tight when the clinician can slide two fingers between the patient and the device. As in applying the camisole, the clinician must have enough assistance and should proceed one step at a time. If possible, at least five clinicians should participate: One clinician to control each of the extremities, and the fifth to actually apply the restraints. The clinician should put the ankle restraints onto the patient first because they are easier to apply than the wrist restraints. After both ankles are restrained, the clinicians can concentrate all available resources on controlling and restraining the wrists. With four-point restraints the clinician must be especially careful of the danger of patient suffocation. Prone restraint upon a soft mattress is dangerous in this respect (the obese are especially at risk in the face-down position upon any surface [cf. Lion & Soloff, 1984]); however, supine restraint carries the risk of the patient's aspiration of vomitus. The position of restraint of the arms will dictate the amount and type of movement available to the patient. Tying both hands to the bed frame at about head level will keep the patient lying down; tying one hand at head level and one at waist level will allow the patient to turn onto one side; and tying both hands at waist level will enable the patient to sit up. The facts of the clinical situation should be considered in reaching a decision about which position to implement. Any emergency restraint must necessarily require constant observation until the patient has been examined by a physician, and has demonstrated an acceptable lessening of agitation and struggling. The patient should ordinarily be released from four-point restraint by first releasing one arm and the contralateral leg and monitoring the patient's psychological adjustment to lessening physical controls (although in an emergency all kinds of restraints can be cut away with scissors, which should always be kept available). When releasing a patient who has been kept recumbent, the clinician must be ready to physically support the patient in the event of orthostatic hypotension.

Other Devices

Other mechanical devices for physically effecting control over the patient have been described. Griffin, Conner, Tait and Warren (1968) reported the use of an animal "tranquilizer gun" to control an extremely agitated, violent psychotic prisoner who had "ripped the bars from the windows, and begun to break through the masonry walls of his cell" (pp. 218–219). Serrill (1985) described two kinds of hand-held electrical "stun guns" which can render humans quickly unconscious. Only time will tell whether the professional mental health community decides that such devices can sometimes be humanely applied to avert potentially hazardous physical confrontations with otherwise unmanageable individuals, or whether their potential for abuse outweighs their possible usefulness.

MEDICATION

Psychotropic medication is a vital therapeutic measure, one which has revolutionized mental health practice. Emergency administration of psychoactive drugs is often indispensable for the safe and effective management of the violent emergency. However, like any other powerful intervention, medication must be administered with a clearly thought out rationale which specifically addresses the behavioral functions for which it is administered. As Lion (1975a) has pointed out, "aggression" is not a clinical entity to be treated directly, but is rather a functional characteristic with a multitude of possible determinants. The symptom of "aggression" must be addressed in terms of its underlying mechanisms. Therefore, there is no medication specifically indicated for "aggression." Nor, of course, should medication be conceptualized apart from other influences upon behavior. Lion also observed that ". . . medication often is mandated with the hope that one or another drug will correct the behavior, as though the behavior could not be influenced by the milieu, by a behavior modification plan, or by simpler verbal interventions" (1983, p. 287). Proper interpersonal technique can enhance the overall behavioral effectiveness of interventions which include medication. For example, Ellman (1984) recommends that the clinician explain that "This medication can help you regain control," and Lion (1983a) notes that "Even flagrantly psychotic patients can comprehend the events around them and should be told what medication they have received and what results are expected" (p. 288).

Medication can be utilized in conjunction with other interventions in order to enable the patient to access the therapeutic effects of the other measures (e.g., verbal and paraverbal communication, seclusion, mechanical restraint). Davis (1985) noted that the restrained patient who demonstrates intractable, frenzied agitation may be at risk of death due to cardiovascular stress or hemorrhage unless medication or ECT can be administered to quell the motoric agitation. Like other intensive interventions (seclusion, restraint), emergency medication is an indication for *increased* rather than decreased involvement with and care for the patient (Lion, 1983a). Medications may be contraindicated in patients who are elderly, or whose disorders are due to unknown etiology or certain organic causes (Tardiff, 1984c). Great care must be taken to recognize side effects and possible interaction of psychotropic medication with other drugs (Tupin, 1983) and possible masking of other medically significant symptoms (Donlon, Hopkin & Tupin, 1979).

Actions and Administration

In general, psychotropic medications have (a) antipsychotic (decreasing hallucination, delusional verbalization, etc.) and/or (b) anxiolytic or sedative (decreasing anxiety, apprehension, arousal, motor activity, etc.) effects upon behavior; particular medications can be characterized in terms of the relative strengths of these kinds of effects (cf. Appelbaum, 1983; Soloff, 1983; Tupin, 1983).

Some medications, such as the benzodiazepines and barbiturates, are utilized specifically because of their anxiolytic or sedative effects. When aggressive behavior is conceptualized as being the result of overwhelming tension or anxiety, such medications may be indicated (cf. Lion, 1983a). Although the major tranquilizers typically have some sedative as well as antipsychotic properties, their use as anxiolytics or sedatives is contraindicated because of their increased incidence of serious side effects and because of the availability of more appropriate drugs, such as barbiturates and benzodiazepines, for such purposes (Appelbaum, 1983; Linden, Davis & Rubinstein, 1982; Lion, 1983a; Mason & Granacher, 1976; Tupin, 1983); however, barbiturates produce CNS depression and can seriously exacerbate existing CNS depression in a patient who has ingested other drugs or who has sustained neurological damage (Tupin, 1983). As Conn and Lion (1984) have noted, benzodiazepines are the medication of choice when agitation is due to alcohol withdrawal (because they are cross-tolerant to alcohol and do not lower seizure threshold) or to PCP intoxication (because they do not aggravate the anticholinergic properties of PCP). The benzodiazepines are typically administered orally or intravenously, because they are poorly and inconsistently absorbed intramuscularly (Davis, 1985; Kutzer & Lion, 1984; Tupin, 1983). Although some authors have suggested that benzodiazepines may lead to a disinhibitory or paradoxical rage reaction (Barry, 1984; Salzman, Kochansky, Shader, Porrino, Harmatz & Swett, 1974; Tupin, 1975, 1983), evidence for such possible reactions is not conclusive (Lion, 1983a).

Rapid Neuroleptization

In recent years, "rapid neuroleptization" has gained widespread acceptance as an emergency medical procedure for intervention with patients whose aggressive behavior is due to psychotic symptomatology (cf. Davis, 1985; Lion, 1983a). Rapid neuroleptization typically consists in the parenteral administration of small amounts of high potency antipsychotic medication, repeated frequently until control of symptoms and behaviors is achieved (Dubin, 1984; Lion, 1983a; Settle, 1984; Zavodnick, 1984). The advantage of the method of rapid neuroleptization is that certain dysfunctional symptoms can be brought under control in a relatively brief period of time (sometimes within three hours [Jacobs, 1983]) by quickly inducing a therapeutic level of medication into the bloodstream. In contrast to oral administration (requiring perhaps 90 minutes for the medication to appear in the bloodstream, and four to six hours for peak level), parenteral administration produces a much more rapid and uniform absorption (in which peak blood level of medication may be achieved within 30 minutes [Settle, 1984]).

Antipsychotic medications can be roughly grouped into "low potency" and "high potency" drugs (effectiveness requiring administration of relatively higher and lower dosages, respectively). Low potency drugs (e.g., chlorpromazine) were in years past used for rapid neuroleptization, but the high potency drugs (e.g., haloperidol) are more commonly used in contemporary practice (Donlon, Hopkin & Tupin, 1979; Lion, 1983a); although haloperidol is most commonly used for rapid neuroleptization, other high potency antipsychotics (fluphenazine, thiothixine, trifluoperazine) are considered equally efficacious to haloperidol and especially appropriate for patients who do not respond adequately to haloperidol or for whom haloperidol is otherwise contraindicated (Barry, 1984; Jacobs, 1983; Lion, 1983a; Settle, 1984). Although the high potency drugs are more likely to produce extrapyramidal side effects than are the low potency drugs, the high potency drugs are also less sedative (an important consideration when level of consciousness is being monitored), less painful at the injection site, less cardiotoxic, less productive of alpha-adrenergic and cholinergic blockade, and less likely to precipitate hypotensive crisis (cf. Donlon, Hopkin & Tupin, 1979; Lion, 1983a; Mason & Granacher, 1976; Rabin & Koomen, 1982; Settle, 1984; Tupin, 1983).

Rapid neuroleptization has been reported to be an effective means of controlling various kinds of psychotic symptoms associated with schizophrenia, affective disorders, organic psychoses, amphetamines, and hallucinogens (Davis, 1985; Donlon, Hopkin & Tupin, 1979; Jacobs, 1983; Mason & Granacher,

1976; Settle, 1984). Rapid neuroleptization is not recommended when the patient suffers ethanol-induced delirium (Zavodnick, 1984), any medical condition for which antipsychotics are contraindicated, or atropine-like psychoses related to anticholinergics such as scopolamine, antihistamines, or tricyclic antidepressants (Mason & Granacher, 1976). Prior to implementing the medication regimen, a comprehensive drug history (including past response to psychotropics, and recently ingested drugs) and physical examination (with special attention to cardiovascular and neurological status) are strongly recommended (Donlon, Hopkin & Tupin, 1979; Mason & Granacher, 1976); special care must be taken with the elderly, the physically infirm, and those suffering delirious and acute brain syndromes (Davis, 1985; Settle, 1982).

There is no clear relationship between the patient's body weight, past requirements for neuroleptic dosage, or severity of impairment, and the optimal dosage of medication (Donlon, Hopkin & Tupin, 1979). Dosage and frequency of administration of antipsychotic medications administered for purposes of rapid neuroleptization must be highly individualized (Donlon, Hopkin & Tupin, 1979; Lion, 1983a; Settle, 1984) and continuously adjusted as a function of the particular patient's pattern of response to the medication. Rapid neuroleptization is not to be confused with "P.R.N. medication," and the ongoing decision making regarding adjustment of dosage and frequency must not be delegated but rather must remain the immediate responsibility of the attending physician (Davis, 1985). However, P.R.N. order for antiparkinsonian agents to be administered at the discretion of others may be appropriate (Davis, 1985; Mason & Granacher, 1976). Authorities recommended intramuscular haloperidol dosages of between 0.5 mg to 30 mg every 30 to 60 minutes up to a maximum total dosage of 30 mg to 100 mg in 24 hours (cf. Davis, 1985; Donlon, Hopkin & Tupin, 1979; Jacobs, 1983; Mason & Granacher, 1976; Tupin, 1983; Walker, 1983; Zavodnick, 1984). It must be emphasized that the effectiveness of the rapid neuroleptization method is due to the quick, precise induction of a therapeutic level of medication into the bloodstream *rather than an excessive level of medication.* There is absolutely no benefit (and perhaps substantial risk) to routine administration of high rather than moderate dosages (Donlon, Hopkin & Tupin, 1979; Ericksen, Hurt & Davis, 1976; Linden, Davis & Rubinstein, 1982). Higher levels of medication should be reserved for only those patients who prove refractory to more customary levels (Donlon, Hopkin & Tupin, 1979; Ericksen, Hurt & Davis, 1976). The physician must have the knowledge, skill, and courage to pursue an aggressive course of symptom control (the tendency of the inexperienced practitioner is typically to undermedicate rather than to overmedicate), yet "snowing" the patient is an ineffective and dangerous practice (Appleton, 1965; Jacobs, 1983). After symptoms have been brought under control, oral medication of the same type given parenterally is recommended for follow-up maintenance (Donlon, Hopkin & Tupin, 1979; Mason & Granacher, 1976; Settle, 1984).

Although rapid neuroleptization is generally safe and effective, possible complications have been noted and clinicians must remain alert for their signs. Extrapyramidal symptoms are among the most common complication to rapid neuroleptization (Donlon, Hopkin & Tupin, 1979; Zavodnick, 1984). Although antiparkinsonian agents may be required to address severe extrapyramidal symptoms, for mild symptoms merely decreasing the amount of antipsychotic medication may suffice: Prophylactic antiparkinsonian medications are not recommended as routine measures during emergency rapid neuroleptization (cf. Mason & Granacher, 1976). Acute dystonias are also common (Mason & Granacher, 1976; Tupin, 1983; Zavodnick, 1984); laryngeal-pharyngeal dystonia constitutes an acute medical emergency because of the threat of respiratory compromise (Davis, 1985; Tupin, 1975). Although less frequent with the high potency antipsychotics, cardiovascular distress and hypotensive episodes are not unknown (Davis, 1985; Mason & Granacher, 1976); blood pressure must be monitored during rapid neuroleptization. Among the more insidious side effects are neuroleptic-induced akinesia or catatonia (Davis, 1985; Zavodnick, 1984) and akathisic violence (Keckich, 1978). In both cases, drug effects may exacerbate or even produce the behaviors for which they are administered, and these increasing symptoms may lead the unwary physician to administer even higher dosages.

Chapter 10

TRAINING ISSUES AND METHODS

Specific training in the methods of psychological and physical crisis intervention serves to protect the patient, the clinician, and the agency within which the patient, the clinician, and others interact. Unfortunately, such training is presently the exception rather than the rule both in training settings and in service settings.

Some appropriate type of training should be available to and required of every person who has contact with patients in the clinical setting. The clinicians whose primary functions involve direct patient care must be thoroughly trained; their supervisors (including Chiefs of Service and others who define policy and standards) should also undergo at least some training in order to ensure that higher-ups are aware of, knowledgeable about, and supportive of patient and clinician problems and the particular methods and technology presented (cf. Gertz, 1980; Lion & Soloff, 1984; Nigrosh, 1983).

There have been obstacles to the widespread adoption of appropriate training, however. Resources are often few and training is a low priority (Gertz, 1980; Snyder, 1983); some clinicians fear that training and an adoption of specific standards for intervention will make them responsible for a more stringent standard of care; and some agencies do not want to acknowledge the problem of patient violence (Nigrosh, 1983). However, appropriate training is essential to protect the welfare of both clinician and patient. The clinician has the responsibility to be adequately trained in order to deal competently with regular demands of clinical practice, and the employing agency has the responsibility to provide the clinician with opportunities and resources for training to cope with the realities of the job. Furthermore, it is likely that as appropriate methods for psychological and physical crisis intervention become more widely disseminated and adopted, such technology will actually become the national "standard of care." The issue of "training negligence" is relevant. Employers have a duty to ensure that employees are adequately trained, and the employer may be liable should outright indifference toward such needs be shown to lead to harm to the patient or the clinician (Belanger & Mullen, 1984; Dyer, Murrell & Wright, 1984). It is conceivable that a clinician who performs intervention procedures without adequate training may be legally answerable to the patient, and that the employing agency that does not provide and insist upon adequate training for its employees may be legally answerable to both the patient and to the clinician (Appelbaum, 1983; Barile, 1982). Both employee unions (cf. Armstrong, 1979; Confederation of Health Service Employees, 1977, 1979) and governmental agencies (cf. LaBrash & Cain, 1984; Lion, Snyder & Merrill, 1981; Nigrosh, 1983) have recognized patient violence as an occupational hazard demanding specialized training; such training has been seen as a means of protecting the civil rights of patients and of early identification of potentially abusive clinicians (cf. Nigrosh, 1983). Training can positively affect the social norms of an institution, inculcating positive values and expectations for appropriate responses to patient aggression (Belanger & Mullen, 1984). Clinicians and organizations alike must come to see specific training in psychological and physical intervention as an asset to everyone concerned: As Nigrosh (1983) has stated,

> Other kinds of physical danger are treated with the utmost respect in health care settings and other facilities which

serve the public. Emergency safety programs aimed, for example, at fire prevention, evacuation, first aid, cardiac emergency care, and water safety receive a great deal of special planning, regulation, training, drilling, and testing. Indications are, however, that in some psychiatric facilities assaults may be the leading cause of injury (p. 266).

In addition to representing sound clinical and administrative practice, training may also prove cost-effective. Lost clinician hours, replacement labor costs (Nigrosh, 1983), and possible insurance premium increases must be factored into the financial equation.

CONTENT OF TRAINING PROGRAMS

In general, the content of training programs should reflect common themes which arise in particular clinical settings, should be consonant with the prevailing treatment philosophy and approach, and should prepare the clinician cognitively, affectively, and behaviorally. Unlike CPR and other emergency-preparedness training programs, there are presently no universally accepted standards for aggression-intervention training programs. Nigrosh (1983) advises careful examination of training curricula, certification procedures for participants, and certification of instructors. In absence of accepted standards, extra care in making training arrangements is necessary.

Among the appropriate objectives for training programs are (a) to acquaint the clinician with relevant legal concepts, (b) to develop the clinician's ability to assess and intervene psychologically, (c) to familiarize the clinician with the indications for, contraindications for, and methods of physical intervention, (d) to build teamwork and to enhance communication among clinicians, (e) to enhance the clinician's confidence in coping with patient aggression, and (f) to positively affect social norms in the professional setting regarding intervention with the aggressive patient. Therefore training programs should include at a minimum (a) an overview of the legal, ethical, and philosophical issues concerning aggressive behavior to serve as a matrix for subsequent information, (b) conceptual models for assessment and intervention, and defusing strategies (c) physical techniques for self-protection and patient-control, (d) simulated situations which allow participants to build professional communications skills, and (e) opportunities for the participant to examine personal and social issues related to managing patient aggression. Training may consist in lecture, readings, group discussion, modeling/simulation, and motor skill development; training aids and materials should be available, as should a mechanism for regular refresher sessions. A criterion-referenced competency examination (including information test and physical performance demonstration) should be administered at the end of training to ensure that objectives have been met at a sufficiently high level to protect both patients and clinicians. Participants should also be given the opportunity to evaluate and make suggestions for improvement of the training program. Of course, it is absolutely unacceptable to present physical methods of intervention in absence of legal, ethical, and social/psychological considerations. A sample training program outline is presented in Appendix 1.

IMPLEMENTING A TRAINING PROGRAM WITHIN AN ORGANIZATION

Successful implementation of training requires a commitment from the highest echelons of the clinical agency to devote adequate resources on an ongoing basis. A one-time training program is unlikely to adequately address the needs of patients, clinicians, or the organization as a whole. Training should be an ongoing process which synergizes clinician and organization, enhancing the performance of each. The specifics of training can be tailored to the unique needs of the patient population served, the clinicians delivering the service, and the agency setting; a general level of familiarization for all staff, and additionally, more specialized training for certain others, is most typically appropriate (Gertz, 1980; Nigrosh, 1983; Piercy, 1984). Training can best be tailored following a "needs assessment" (cf. Smith & Delahaye, 1983). This procedure should include sampling of information regarding the patient population, frequency and types of aggressive behavior, clinician attitudes and knowledge, and organizational procedures. In accordance with both needs and resources, training has been successfully implemented in a variety of formats ranging from brief yearly in-service training (of perhaps one or two days) with periodic refresher sessions, to intensive skill development modules (of up to several weeks) with constant "refresher" practice (cf. Barile, 1982; Fein, Gareri & Hansen, 1981; Gertz, 1980; Kronberg, 1983; Lehmann et al., 1983; Nigrosh, 1983; "Program . . . ," 1976; Ramirez, Bruce & Whaley, 1981; Snyder, 1983). Such programs can be a regular part of a new clinician's orientation training upon employment.

An interdisciplinary task force (with representatives from each professional clinical discipline, and from administrative/ clerical, legal, maintenance, security, patient, public, and other sectors as appropriate) should oversee and approve the training program curriculum, and formulate written policies and procedures regarding training and the appropriate clinical management of patient aggression.

It is important to distinguish participants in a training program from instructors, who in turn must be distinguished from instructors-in-chief (cf. Nigrosh, 1983): Participants receive the training but are not ordinarily considered qualified by such an experience to train others adequately. Instructors are considered competent to train others in the specific methods in which they have been trained, yet not to train new instructors independently. Instructors-in-chief are considered qualified to train instructors, and also to develop new clinical intervention methods and to exercise overall responsibility for training programs. Although there are no nationally accepted standards defining the minimum qualifications of prospective instructors in this area, a few reasonable criteria can be offered.

First, because the training essentially involves presentation of sophisticated principles and procedures for clinical intervention, the instructor-in-chief must be a Qualified Mental Health Professional, duly trained and accredited for the independent practice of a recognized professional clinical discipline. Some persons with a highly developed degree of physical skill and perhaps even extensive training experience may prove to be invaluable technical assistants and may perform the bulk of actual instruction, but one who would not otherwise be qualified for a senior level of clinical practice or instruction should not be considered for overall leadership of such a training program any more than a psychiatric aide with exquisite and effective interpersonal skills gained through years of experience would be considered qualified as the independent head of a clinical treatment team. Individuals with less than senior clinical credentials may qualify as instructors, provided that they meet the remainder of the criteria. Instructor teams are highly recommended, so that each individual can compensate for gaps in the other's ability, experience, and qualifications; such an arrangement also prevents instructor exhaustion and provides a change of pace to alleviate participant boredom.

Second, the prospective instructor must be an experienced clinician who has the respect of colleagues (cf. Belanger & Mullen, 1984). Without such qualifications, an instructor cannot be a credible source of information even though factually knowledgeable.

Third, the prospective instructor must undergo a thorough training program. It must be emphasized that although successful completion of the actual course may be one prerequisite for becoming an instructor, additional specialized training specifically for development of instructional competence is essential (cf. Nigrosh, 1983). Under the continuing supervision and evaluation of an instructor-in-chief, a prospective instructor should proceed from assisting another instructor who is teaching a course, to teaching a course assisted and observed by another instructor, to teaching under close supervision, to teaching with relative independence under the overall guidance of an instructor-in-chief.

Fourth, the prospective instructor must have a sincere interest in and make a commitment to training others. Because of the resources required for instructor training, the instructor who does not train other clinicians represents a poor investment of time and energy. In order to gain the necessary technical expertise, an organization (or consortium of organizations) may want to retain the services of a qualified consultant in order to begin the training process.

GENERAL POINTS OF INSTRUCTIONAL TECHNIQUE

Effective training is a demanding skill: Mere mastery of the content area is in no way an adequate substitute for adequate preparation in the methods and techniques of instruction. Practice of lectures and demonstrations (even before empty lecture halls!) is remarkably effective, as is routine audiotaping or videotaping of the instructors' actual training sessions for review and feedback about instructional technique and effectiveness.

Overview

Specific objectives must be identified for the training: Objectives are concrete statements about what the participant will be able to do following training. The initial needs assessment will help to determine appropriate objectives which will remedy identified deficiencies in knowledge, attitude, or skill. Objectives should be integrated into a structured overall plan, with specific instructional methods and a timetable. A modular training format, in which one or perhaps two circumscribed objectives are addressed during each module, is a most versatile method. Modules can be presented independently during brief training sessions, or linked into longer sessions. Because distributed practice is superior to massed practice, a number of brief training sessions is preferable to a single, long session. Whether the participant may attend one module without attending others should be clarified in advance.

Unaugmented verbal presentation of material is typically the least effective and least motivating instructional method. Spoken communications must be made simple, and must be repeated often for clarity and retention. Presentations involving multiple senses are vastly preferable. Projected transparencies, charts, videotapes, and the like give added impact and clarity to spoken communications. Activities such as group discussion, simulation, and physical demonstration and exercises are exciting; because they involve the participant directly, such activities are usually much more effective than lectures and are excellent means of illustrating principles presented during lectures and of building group cohesion and countering fatigue and boredom. A written syllabus, with a sketch of topics and times, can help to give participants an overall structure for understanding specific material presented; a workbook in outline format will facilitate note taking (unfortunately, expository text will encourage the participant to read during the session rather than participate).

Following lecture periods, large groups can be broken down into subgroups, facilitating discussion, exercises, and close supervision of individuals. On the whole, relative strangers rather than friends should be placed together because groups of strangers tend to remain more formally task-oriented. One participant from each group should be designated "recording secretary" to take notes and to describe process, experiences, and observations when the subgroups reconvene into the larger group. Such a procedure will also ensure that subgroups stay on-task in the absence of the instructor.

Review and practice are essential. Material should be reviewed the end of each module; reviews are also an excellent way to begin subsequent modules. Each module should also have an evaluation component to determine whether instructional objectives have been met in terms of objective criteria. Objectives which have been clearly stated in terms of action verbs will be the easiest to measure; common measurement methods include written tests to measure knowledge, questionnaires to measure attitude, and actual demonstration during simulation exercises to measure physical performance skill. As a means to enhance motivation and to identify participants who have achieved competency, certificates should be awarded at the end of training to those who meet the instructional objective criteria.

Variables related to the training facility itself are critical for the success of instruction. The training area should be evaluated carefully in terms of physical size, temperature, acoustics, and freedom from distraction. A carpeted floor is a definite asset for physical skills training. Seating arrangements must be conducive to the kinds of interactions which are required for training. Large auditoria with fixed, front-facing seats are not suitable for this type of instruction; gymnasia and large halls must be carefully evaluated acoustically. Finally, the time of day and the day of week scheduled for training is an often overlooked influence. Sessions must not be scheduled at times when participants are too exhausted or too harried to make use of the presentation.

Breaking the Ice

The first few minutes of a training session can set the tone for the remainder of the instruction; early rapport is critical for success. At the time of registration, participants should be asked to complete a background questionnaire, asking for name, professional discipline and experience, and (a) their goals and expectations of the training, and (b) a description of one violent incident which they have experienced, witnessed, or heard about from colleagues. These procedures will help to orient the participants and set a task-oriented expectation from the outset. In a relatively small group, it is often helpful to have participants interview one another briefly at the beginning of the first session, and then individually to introduce their fellow participant to the rest of the group, stating the participant's name, professional background, and training goals. It is also helpful for the instructor to make a brief comment or ask a question of each participant following the introduction. Such procedures lead to more detailed sharing of information to the group as a whole than is typically the case when participants introduce themselves; it also fosters feelings of acceptance and group cohesion.

Utilization of Questioning

Skillful questioning and handling of participants' questions can greatly enhance the effectiveness of the training sessions, and can be used as a method to direct and guide group discussion, case analysis, simulations, and the like (cf. Smith & Delahaye, 1983). There are four main types of questions asked by the instructor: (a) the overhead question, asked of the group as a whole, (b) the direct question, asked of a particular participant, (c) the funnel question, which begins in an open-ended fashion and becomes progressively narrower in focus in order to guide the participants' thoughts, and (d) the relay question, in which one participant's answer serves as the basis for a question to be asked of another participant. Insofar as possible, questions should be constructed so as to elicit a discovery process among the participants. In general, closed-ended questions with brief, specific answers should be avoided unless the instructor intends to follow the answer with a request for the respondent to explain the answer further. In the initial stages of the training, the instructor should ask questions with a high probability of being answered correctly in order to build rapport and participant confidence. In the event of incorrect answers, the instructor should acknowledge the effort in answering, highlight any correct part of the answer, and rephrase the question or break it down into smaller parts in order to eventually elicit a correct answer. The instructor should then "reflect" the answer, using different words to ensure that the participant fully understands the concept underlying the answer. If some participants rarely answer questions, their participation may be increased by asking them direct yet easily answered questions; when some participants attempt to answer a disproportionate share of overhead questions, the instructor should ask direct questions of different participants. Questions directed to the instructor may be profitably handled by relaying them to different participants so that they can develop the correct answer.

Simulation

Simulation can be an exceptionally valuable training technique because, in contrast to hearing about, reading about, discussing or watching, participants can actually experience approximations to real situations in which skills and concepts can be developed in a safe environment with appropriate feedback and supervision. It is the preferred instructional modality for developing the participants' ability to apply principles and develop techniques, and to allow participants to explore and alter feelings and attitudes (cf. Barile, 1982; DiFabio & Ackerhalt, 1978; Nigrosh, 1983; Smith & Delahaye, 1983).

Because simulation requires a basic level of trust among participants and between instructor and participants, these modalities should not be attempted prematurely; rapport is essential. Among the most successful simulations are those suggested by the participants from actual case material. In large groups where not every participant can take direct part in a simulation, the instructor may (a) have the group nominate players with nonparticipants observing the simulation, or (b) divide the group into subgroups which can either enact simultaneous simulations or serially present the simulations for other subgroups to observe. The smallest workable subgroup is generally composed of three participants, with at least two interacting with a third observing (the observer formalizes the situation and keeps the process on-task).

Although simulation should not be treated frivolously, neither should it become inappropriately serious, as emotional and interpersonal difficulties can ensue. It is the instructor's responsibility to monitor the process closely and to intervene if necessary. Simulations are most productive when the instructor stops the action at strategic points to ask the group to suggest strategy, to give participants a chance to replay or modify a portion of the simulation, or to elicit or highlight relevant principles. Following simulation, the instructor should emphasize positive aspects and successes which were demonstrated. Should discussion digress or become destructive, the instructor should interrupt with a question, summarize, or call a brief recess.

Problem Participants

Although a well prepared and competently delivered training program will keep inappropriate behavior by participants to a minimum, the instructor must be prepared to cope with problems should they arise.

The instructor should begin by ensuring that the content and style of presentation of the program are appropriate for the given audience. A pretest of knowledge can help the instructor to gauge the participants' needs, can sensitize the participants to their need to learn the material, and can also help to establish the instructor's expertise and credibility. Expectations for participant involvement and cooperation should be positively addressed at the initial session, and resistance can be re-framed as an expected part of learning new material and a normal, typical part of the learning process.

The individual participant who persistently presents a problem should be identified early and appropriate steps taken to address that participant's motivations and concerns. If a brief, direct conversation during a break does not resolve the difficulty, group dynamics can become the instructor's ally. Other participants—especially those perceived as high-status or as leaders—may be asked to respond to the disrupter's inappropriate questions or to comment upon the disrupter's behavior; the group as a whole will typically exert pressure upon a disruptor to conform to a task-oriented norm.

TRAINING EXERCISES

The following training exercises illustrate various psychological and physical principles, and give training participants simulation experience for skill-building practice.

Psychological Training Exercises

The following exercises can complement lectures and didactic sessions which present theoretical material. These exercises can give an experiential context for understanding conceptual issues, and can facilitate learning and retention.

1. In a group, participants describe violent professional situations they have experienced and their personal reactions to these situations; these descriptions are then analyzed for underlying principles, precipitants, possible responses; common dimensions of personal reactions; legal principles; etc.

2. In a group, participants describe violent professional situations they have experienced. These situations are used for simulation, with the person describing the incident assigning roles and observing the interaction. Following the simulation, process the interaction from the point of view of the patient,

of the clinician, and of the observer. Attempt to find superior solutions to the problem depicted and implement them in a follow-up simulation.

3. In triads, for one minute (timed by the observer) one participant describes to another a personal event which was very emotionally positive; at the end of the minute the listener attempts to recount in exact detail the speaker's description. All three persons should have an opportunity to describe and to listen. This exercise demonstrates one's personal reactions and the internal "noise" which make it difficult to fully concentrate on another's communications. Participants can describe to the larger group their experiences in attempting to attend to the other's story.

4. Triads of participants perform the "Impasse Perception Validation Algorithm." One participant describes the impasse and observes as the other two attempt to check perceptions and reach a resolution using the algorithm.

5. Triads of participants practice the direct and indirect methods of limit-setting. One participant describes the behavior needing limitation and observes as the other two enact first the direct and then the indirect procedure.

6. A group of participants develops a set of policies and procedures for their agency, as a means of developing their understanding of the underlying principles.

7. Participants watch videotapes of simulations without the sound, in order to sharpen skills in analyzing nonverbal behaviors.

8. With two long lines of participants facing one another, perform the following to observe another's reactions and to illustrate nonverbal behavior principles; perform the exercises with a variety of persons differing in age, gender, race, demeanor, size, etc.: (a) Participants stare without blinking into one another's eyes. What is communicated, and how? What reactions does each have, and what do they mean? (b) One line of participants stands still while the second approaches gradually. At what distance does comfort become discomfort? How is a straight approach different than an angular or from-behind approach? Is approaching different from being approached? (c) One participant approaches another directly, full-facing un-

til the participant being approached feels discomfort and tells the approacher to stop; after a brief while the approacher keeps the same distance but turns side-facing the other person. Does this change the feeling of comfort/discomfort for either? (d) Participants attempt nonverbally to convey either threat or appeasement to one another. How is this conveyed? What cues make the communication seem credible or artificial?

9. In a group, some participants close their eyes. Others roam about and each secretly touches one eyes-closed participant lightly on the shoulder. Participants who had closed their eyes later attempt to determine which person touched them. This exercise highlights observational skills and subtleties of nonverbal behavior (eye contact, posture, attempts at dissimulation, etc.).

10. As homework, participants are asked to attempt the following, to observe reactions, and to describe the relevant principles of nonverbal behavior: (a) stare at a friend's eyes without blinking during casual conversation, (b) while standing in casual conversation with a friend, first stand too close and later stand too far, (c) follow strangers too closely in a hall, (d) in an elevator, turn to face the other riders, (e) when other empty seats are available, sit directly next to another person at a cafeteria, library, bus, theater, etc.

Physical Training Exercises

Special requirements for physical training. Because of the unique nature of physical training, some special requirements must be met before attempting these exercises.

Emphasis must be maintained upon the concept of physical intervention as a procedure for *therapeutic* intervention and its meaning to the patient. The instructor should attempt to elicit and process participants' attitudes and feelings that may be made especially accessible during physical training sessions. The psychological components of physical intervention will be made apparent when a participant attempts to gain release from a practice partner who is prepared for an escape attempt. Such an attempt usually does not succeed because the partner is not surprised, unlike actual situations in which the patient's attention is not focused totally upon the mechanics of the attack and in which the patient does not expect a precipitous defensive maneuver. No technique can be "proven" or "disproven" during practice sessions because the psychological realities of an actual therapeutic physical intervention cannot be fully recreated during training sessions.

Responsibility for one's own well-being and for the safety of one's training partner must be repeatedly emphasized. Physical training need be neither rough nor dangerous. Participants must be screened so that those with either psychological or physical contraindications to the training can be asked to observe rather than to participate as hands-on learners. The instructor must be absolutely noncoercive about whether an individual chooses to participate in or merely to observe the physical training session; additionally, the instructor is advised to have participants sign a "release from liability" before physical training. Although many attorneys suggest that such a release is scant protection in a court of law, the instructor may significantly decrease the chances of being sued in the first place when participants have been given a free choice about taking part and have agreed not to hold the instructor responsible for any inadvertent injuries. A sample release form is presented in Appendix 2.

The following "safe practice rules" must always be observed; they must be thoroughly discussed, and reiterated before each and every physical practice session.

1. The physical training environment must be adequate, and free from potentially hazardous objects and characteristics.

2. Participants must wear appropriate attire, and remove jewelry and adornments which might possibly injure the participant or partners (e.g., belt buckles, earrings, pens, watches). Aspects which cannot be modified (e.g., eyeglasses, long fingernails) should receive special cautionary attention. If participants do not have safe footwear, removal of shoes (and stockings also if working upon slippery floor surface) is recommended.

3. Participants must practice only those maneuvers immediately presented by the instructor, going slowly and gently at first and increasing speed and firmness only as skill is acquired and always within the limits of safety for both participant and

partner. Participants must not use too much force nor resist too strenuously when the partner is attempting to learn to perform a new technique.

4. Participants must be certain that their partner is ready before attempting any physical maneuver, and must immediately terminate all physical activity when the instructor or training partner says, "Stop!" This specific watchword must be obeyed absolutely to prevent inadvertent injury.

5. In order to maintain attention to task and a safe attitude, participants must defer questions that begin with "But what if . . ." and instead concentrate on learning the demonstrated maneuvers thoroughly. Following the presentation of all standard maneuvers and techniques, the instructor should give participants the opportunity to ask about novel or unusual situations. However, rather than attempting to answer such questions, the instructor should instead relay the question to the rest of the group in order to give them supervised experience in applying the principles to unexpected situations.

Physical maneuvers should be taught and reviewed in small steps which are practiced to mastery. These small components can then be combined to form more complex techniques. Most participant learning difficulties can be traced to steps which are too large for the participant to assimilate. As with other types of learning, distributed practice is superior to massed practice. A number of brief training sessions is better than one or two long sessions. Frequent reviews are also recommended, especially at the beginning of a new session and upon completion of an instructional unit. Physical training exercises are an excellent method to combat drowsiness (after lunch, or in the late afternoon) and to refresh lagging attention at other times.

The instructor should refrain from demonstrating escapes and restraints upon the participants. The goal of training is to enable the participants to learn to apply principles, and to enhance their confidence in coping. Participants may feel inadequate and less confident when their attempts to perform maneuvers are compared to those of the instructor. Instead, the instructor should play the role of the "patient" during demonstration and the participant should be slowly and gently guided in the right direction, resulting in a success experience.

All of the *principles* of physical intervention should be demonstrated and thoroughly understood by participants before the instructor presents any *applied techniques*, to ensure that the participant develops adequate understanding and the ability to adapt appropriately to novel situations, rather than mere rote learning. New techniques should be demonstrated slowly, one step at a time, and the components should be described thoroughly as the instructor guides the participants' actions. The instructor should not directly criticize the participants' actions unless they are dangerous or overaggressive, but instead should focus on enhancing the positive aspects of the performance and encouraging the participants to explore alternatives to inferior aspects of performance. Visual aids (slides or illustrations) can help the participants gain an overview of the maneuvers, and videotape of the participants can give direct, immediate feedback. After the participants achieve basic skill, the instructor should explore the components that the participants found most difficult to accomplish, and should inquire whether any participant has discovered a superior method. Perhaps a better technique will emerge, but more commonly the participants will gain valuable practice in critical conceptual analysis of physical intervention procedures. In any event, the instructor must never let a "challenge" situation develop in which a participant attempts to demonstrate a special attack, defense, or restraint maneuver in an antagonistic or nonhelpful manner. Competency in the physical techniques can be measured in terms of specific performance criteria (does the participant attempt to escape from grasp by going against patient's thumb rather than against fingers; does the participant tuck the chin to protect the throat in response to an arm-bar choke from behind). The particular techniques and responses considered essential for minimal competence will vary as a function of setting. Finally, periodic practice and review on a formalized basis are essential, although the frequency and intensity of such reviews will also vary as a function of setting.

Specific exercises. The following exercises are primarily intended to serve as means of illustrating the *principles* underlying the applied techniques of physical intervention. In addition to the following exercises, participants should of course be thoroughly instructed in the prototypical applied techniques described in previous chapters.

1. Use overhead questioning to elicit from participants (a) the requirements for acceptable professional physical intervention techniques, (b) the principles underlying the effectiveness of the professional physical intervention techniques, (c) the realistic limitations of physical intervention techniques, and (d) the safe practice rules.

2. After teaching the method to escape from a simple one-hand wrist grab, demonstrate the importance of attentional distraction by pairing two participants of approximately equal strength. Have one grab the other at the wrist, and tell the grabbing partner not to let the other participant out of the grab; while the grabbing partner is paying attention, escape may be difficult or impossible. Then whisper into the ear of the participant being grabbed the directive to make a surprising, precipitous release attempt when the instructor whispers into the other partner's ear. The instructor then begins to whisper into the grabbing partner's ear, ostensibly to give similar instructions. However, when the grabbing partner's attention is upon the instructor's whispering, the grabbed partner makes a sudden escape.

3. Participants can be shown that it is impossible to implement a defense (or an attack) faster than a person can react. Participants pair up. One participant holds hands up, palms facing forward. The other partner places an index finger against the other participant's chest or stomach. The partner doing the poking will attempt to push the finger sharply against the other participant *only when the poking partner sees the other participant begin to move the upheld hands.* The participant being poked can almost always precipitously and swiftly bat the poking partner's hand away before the partner can react with an attempt to poke.

4. Participants are instructed that even in the event of a strong choke hold from a patient, they can expect to have perhaps 10 seconds to react defensively before losing consciousness. The participants are instructed to close their eyes and imagine themselves being choked. The instructor then times 10 full seconds. Most participants will feel that this 10-second pe-

riod is actually a long time, and that although they may initially panic, they will find that there is sufficient time to recover from that reaction and to effect the proper self-protection maneuver.

5. Participants are asked to assess their own attire (including footwear and jewelry) in terms of its likely effect upon an unexpected need for physical intervention with a patient; they also observe the immediate instructional setting for objects which can potentially be used as weapons or as defensive shields.

6. Participants hold both hands palm open near the ears. Upon the instructor's precipitous signal "Now!" the participants attempt to bring the hands toward the stomach as fast as possible. After a few repetitions of this exercise, the opposite is tried. Participants attempt to raise the hands from a position near the stomach to protect the head. Of course, the hands travel much more quickly from the head toward the midsection. The relevance of this principle for blocking blows and protecting the head should be stressed.

7. Principles of leverage can be demonstrated by (a) having one participant hold one arm straight out in front in a punch-like posture, and having another partner attempt to move the participant's arm first by pressing near the partner's shoulder and second by pressing near the partner's wrist, and (b) having one participant stand with arms at side and having partner stand behind and attempt to prevent participant from raising arms outward from side, first by holding participant's arms near shoulder, then by holding participant's arms at elbow joint.

8. Participants should attempt to define positions of maximum arm strength by lifting one another under the axillae (a) by holding with hand, elbow straight, (b) by holding with hand, elbow bent, and (c) by holding in crook of elbow, elbow bent.

9. The difference between mechanically strong and weak body positions can be demonstrated by having participants make an imaginary grabbing motion, arm straight, fist clenched (a) palm upward, first as far below the waist as possible and then slowly raising the arm to a position above the head, and then (b) palm downward, first above the head and then slowly lowering the arm to a position as far below the waist as possible. The palm-upward grab has maximal strength low and

minimal strength high; the reverse is true for the palm-downward grab.

10. The principles of effective use of body weight and utilization of the anaerobic cycle can be demonstrated by having one participant grab the other in a bear hug and lift the participant off the floor. The participant need do nothing other than relax, thus making effective use of body weight in lieu of muscular strength; meanwhile, the partner is becoming anaerobically tired from holding the participant.

11. Participants can become sensitized to the mechanics and dynamics of proper stance. First, participants roll their hips in wide circles (as in a hula hoop) while varying the parameters of the stance: While circling the hips, the participants place their feet very close together, very far apart, or about shoulder width; the participants keep weight on heels or on balls of feet; the participants keep knees locked straight or slightly bent. Participants then attempt to describe principles governing the stance. Pairs of participants then assume a stance with a shoulder's width between the feet, facing one another at about arm's length first frontally and then sideways. In each orientation, participants attempt to (a) push one another back, and then (b) lean away from one another. The sideways orientation should be found to be clearly superior for both pushing and for leaning away from the partner.

12. Participants should be sensitized to the "safety zones" and the "danger zones." In pairs, one participant attempts to remain as close as possible while still remaining outside the danger zone; the partner then fakes punches, kicks, and lunges at the participant. The partcipant should experience the different distances required to remain in the distal safety zone when standing in front of, at the side of, and behind the partner. The participant should also discover whether standing frontally or side-facing allows greater mobility for retreat from attack.

13. Participants should practice monitoring eye contact and gaze in a nonobtrusive manner. One participant playing the role of "patient" faces two or more partners playing "clinicians." The participant will attempt to precipitously punch, kick, or lunge toward one of the other partners without warning but will look at the person first, gazing low for a lower attack and high for

a higher attack. The participants must unobtrusively monitor the partner's gaze and be ready to make a defensive or evasive action.

14. The pivoting principle can be illustrated by having one participant attempt to get chest to chest against a partner as in an aggressive confrontation by a patient against a clinician; rather than standing firm or backing up, the partner reacts to the confrontation by pivoting, leaving the front foot in place and sliding the back foot behind in a circular pattern. A repeated series of pivots will actually move the partner in a backwards circle, pivoting around the frontmost foot, thus avoiding direct bodily confrontation with the participant while neither standing firm nor backing straight up.

15. The principle of avoiding the opposition of force can be illustrated in an exercise whereby one participant extends a straight arm, fist clenched, in a slow punchlike action. The partner (a) attempts to stop the punch by pressing with the palm directly against the participant's fist against the direction of the punch, (b) attempts to guide the punch away by pressing the palm directly against the fist and moving the fist around in a circular motion, and then (c) attempts to deflect the punch by pressing with the palm obliquely against the participant's arm near the wrist of the punching hand. Alternatives (b) and (c) are obviously more effective than (a) because they do not entail direct opposition to force.

16. After the physical techniquess have been thoroughly practiced, one participant faces a line of other partners: The partners approach the participant serially, one at a time, and deliver unrehearsed attacks so that the participant gets an opportunity to practice responding instantly.

17. Various soft objects can be used to simulate attacks. For example, a pillow can simulate an attack with a chair, a foam ball can be thrown to simulate a glass ashtray or other object, and marking pens (with water-based, washable ink) can be used to simulate knife attacks.

18. Among the most useful simulations involving physical intervention techniques are situations involving seclusion, manual restraint, and mechanical restraint. Such simulations build teamwork and communication skills as well as physical compe-

tence. It is often useful to have clinicians reverse roles (physician plays psychiatric technician, nurse plays physician) in order to sensitize participants to the unique demands of other disciplines and in order to elicit unrecognized and perhaps nonconsensual expectations. Every clinician should have the firsthand experience of being cornered, being the object of intervention by a group of clinicians, being secluded, being manually restrained, and being mechanically restrained, in order to understand the basis for the effect of the techniques and in order to build empathy for the experience of the patient (cf. Fein, Gareri & Hansen, 1981; Nigrosh, 1983).

Appendix 1

SAMPLE TRAINING PROGRAM

THERAPEUTICS FOR AGGRESSION

Description

Therapeutics for Aggression is a comprehensive, integrated system of psychological and physical principles allowing the clinician to assess and intervene in violent crisis situations while safely and humanely protecting the self and others. Lecture, small group discussion, simulation, and physical demonstration are used to teach components of this system. Length of training program: 8 to 40 hours. Participants should be comfortably attired, and have functional footwear.

Instructor

Michael Thackrey completed his doctorate in clinical psychology at Vanderbilt University in Nashville, TN, and a postdoctoral fellowship at the Vanderbilt Center for Psychotherapy Research. Formerly Director of the Community Crisis Center in Altoona, PA, Dr. Thackrey is presently Clinical Director of

Sumner Mental Health Services in Gallatin, TN, and Adjunct Assistant Professor of Psychology at Vanderbilt.

Target Audience

For professional clinicians of all disciplines who work directly with patients; who educate, consult to, or supervise direct-service clinicians; or who set clinical policy and standards.

Objectives

Upon completion of the training program, each participant will be able to:

(1) Describe and utilize psychological principles for violent emergency assessment and intervention (measured by observed simulation and written instrument);
(2) Recognize related critical legal concepts (measured by written instrument);
(3) Identify and demonstrate safe, effective, humane physical intervention procedures (measured by observed simulation and written instrument);
(4) Identify essential requirements for training programs in this area (measured by written instrument).

Certificates will be awarded to persons successfully passing examinations.

Training Materials

(1) Training workbook;
(2) Reprints of journal articles and similar materials;
(3) Annotated bibliography.

Training Modules

(1) Introduction and overview (preview; epidemiology)
(2) Philosophical and ethical issues in managing aggression

(personal and professional aspects of managing aggression; necessity of training; purpose of intervention)

(3) Legal issues in managing aggression (appropriate treatment and standard of care; least restrictive alternative; emergency measures; abuse)

(4) Psychological principles I (biobehavioral systems; crisis intervention theory)

(5) Physical principles I (psychological aspects)

(6) Psychological principles II (nature of aggressive behavior; verbal and nonverbal communication; assessment/ intervention matrix)

(7) Physical principles II (anatomical/physiological/mechanical aspects)

(8) Psychological techniques I (crisis conflict negotiation, direct and indirect limit-setting technology)

(9) Physical techniques I (humane, nonabusive self-preservation)

(10) Psychological techniques II (teamwork and group intervention)

(11) Physical techniques II (patient restraint and transportation)

(12) Emergency psychopharmacology (rapid neuroleptization)

(13) Organizational issues in managing aggression (acceptance of problem, commitment to resource allocation, written policy)

(14) Instructional techniques and continuing education resources (implementing training programs)

(15) Review

(16) Participant examination and course evaluation

(17) Awarding of certificates and closing

Appendix 2

SAMPLE RELEASE FROM
LIABILITY FORM

RELEASE FROM LIABILITY

This release from liability is made between Michael Thackrey and: name of Participant: _____ (hereinafter "Participant") with regard to a training program described as *Therapeutics for Aggression* by Michael Thackrey.

Specifically, Participant understands that Michael Thackrey in addition to providing lectures, discussions, simulations, and role-play opportunities will demonstrate and involve Participant and others in physical intervention techniques and maneuvers. These physical techniques and maneuvers will be demonstrated and practiced by Participant and others, as well as by Michael Thackrey, as a part of the *Therapeutics for Aggression* training program.

Participant is aware of and understands that the physical techniques and maneuvers involve physical contact and include risk of injury to Participant and loss or damage of Participant's property. Participant's involvement in the physical techniques and maneuvers is entirely voluntary, and Participant understands that he or she may refuse to undertake all or part of the physical techniques and maneuvers portion of the training program without loss and understands that such refusal is his or her sole right. Such refusal to undertake the physical techniques and maneuvers portion of the training program shall in no way be deemed to affect adversely Participant's meeting of criteria or requirements for successful completion of the training program.

Participant accepts risk of injury, damage, and loss of property and freely agrees not to hold Michael Thackrey and his agents, other Participants, or anyone else individually or collectively responsible for any or all injury to Participant or damage to or loss of any kind which may be sustained as a consequence of the physical techniques and maneuvers portion of the training program. Participant agrees to release and discharge Michael Thackrey and his agents, other Participants, and all other persons from any and all liability for any and all injury, damage, or loss arising out of Participant's undertaking the physical techniques and maneuvers, and further agrees to hold harmless Michael Thackrey and his agents, other Participants, and all other persons from any and all claims, demands, judgments, executions, or other action for any injury, damage, or loss.

If Participant does engage in the physical techniques and maneuvers portion of the training, however, he or she warrants that his or her personal medical condition at the time of training, whether known or unknown, shall not be grounds for any claim, demand, judgment, execution, or other action against any of those named above.

Participant understands that although the physical techniques and maneuvers may be effective procedures for intervening with emotionally disturbed or mentally retarded persons, Participant assumes full responsibility for any injury, damage, or loss resulting from application or employment of these techniques in any setting whatsoever. Michael Thackrey makes no warranty of any kind that the techniques presented will prevent or avoid injury, damage, or loss of any kind either to Participant or to any other persons or parties.

Michael Thackrey   Participant
Signature: Signature:
Date: Date:

CORRESPONDENCE

The author is interested in corresponding with other persons regarding issues in the therapeutic management of patient aggression:

Michael Thackrey, Ph.D.
Sumner Mental Health Services
Post Office Box 8047
Gallatin, TN 37066
-or-
Department of Psychology
College of Arts & Science
Vanderbilt University
Nashville, TN 37240

BIBLIOGRAPHY

Abbott, A. (1978). Accident and its correlates in a psychiatric hospital. *Acta Psychiatrica Scandinavica, 57*, 36-48.

Abroms, G. M. (1968). Setting limits. *Archives of General Psychiatry, 19*, 113-119.

Abusive patients: Nurses emotional reactions. (1982). *Regan Report on Nursing Law, 22* (12).

Addad, M., Benezech, M., Bourgeois, M. & Yesavage, J. (1981). Criminal acts among schizophrenics in French mental hospitals. *Journal of Nervous and Mental Disease, 169*, 289-293.

Adler, G. & Shapiro L. N. (1973). Some difficulties in the treatment of the aggressive acting-out patient. *American Journal of Psychotherapy, 27*, 548-557.

Adler, W. N., Kreeger, C. & Ziegler, P. (1983). Patient violence in a private psychiatric hospital. In J. R. Lion & W. H. Reid (Eds.), *Assaults within psychiatric facilities* (pp. 81-89). New York: Grune & Stratton.

Albee, G. W. (1950). Patterns of aggression in psychopathology. *Journal of Consulting Psychology, 14*, 465-468.

Allison, C. & Bale, R. (1973). A hospital policy for the care of patients who exhibit violent behavior. *Nursing Times, 69*, 375-377.

American Psychiatric Association. (1985). *Seclusion and restraint: The psychiatric uses* (Task Force Report No. 22). Washington, DC: American Psychiatric Association.

Anders, R. L. (1977). When a patient becomes violent. *American Journal of Nursing, 77*, 1144-1148.

Anders, R. L. (1980). Management of violent patients. *Critical Care Update, 7* (11), 5-8, 10-11, 14-15.

Andrade, P. D. & Andrade, J. C. (1979). Professional liability of the psychiatric nurse. *Journal of Psychiatry & Law, 7*, 141-186.

Annis, L. V., McClaren, H. A. & Baker, C. A. (1984). Who kills us? Case study of a clinician's murderer. In J. T. Turner (Ed.), *Violence in the health care setting: A survival guide*. Rockville, MD: Aspen.

APA task force issues guidelines for use of seclusion and restraint in inpatient settings. (1985). *Hospital & Community Psychiatry, 36*, 677, 679.

Appelbaum, P. S. (1983). Legal considerations in the prevention and treatment of assault. In J. R. Lion & W. H. Reid (Eds.), *Assaults within psychiatric facilities* (pp. 173-190). New York: Grune & Stratton.

Appelbaum, P. S. (1984). Legal issues. In F. G. Guggenheim & M. F. Weiner (Eds.), *Manual of psychiatric consultation and emergency care* (pp. 101-110). New York: Jason Aronson.

Appelbaum, P. S., Jackson, A. H. & Shader, R. I. (1983). Psychiatrists' responses to violence: Pharmacologic management of psychiatric inpatients. *American Journal of Psychiatry, 140*, 301-304.

Appelbaum, P. S., Leeman, C. P., Peele, R. & Bachrach, L. L. (1980). Least restrictive environment: Some comments, amplification. *Hospital & Community Psychiatry, 31*, 420-422.

Appleton, W. S. (1965). The snow phenomenon: Tranquilizing the assaultive. *Psychiatry, 28*, 88-93.

Ardrey, R. (1966). *The territorial imperative: A personal inquiry into the animal origins of property and nations*. New York: Atheneum.

Armstrong, B. (1978). Handling the violent patient in the hospital. *Hospital & Community Psychiatry, 29*, 463-467.

Armstrong, B. (1979). A question of abuse: Where staff and patient rights collide. *Hospital & Community Psychiatry, 30*, 348-351.

Askenasy, J. J., Hackett, P. P., Ron, S. & Hary, D. (1983). Violence and episodic behavioral dyscontrol. *Biological Psychiatry, 18*, 604-607.

Assaults in hospitals: Nurses and patients. (1981). *Regan Report on Nursing Law, 22* (7).

Aston, C. C. (1980). Restrictions encountered in responding to terrorist sieges: An analysis. In R. H. Shultz, Jr. & S. Sloan (Eds.), *Responding to the terrorist threat: Security and crisis management* (pp. 59-92). New York: Pergamon.

Atkinson, J. H. (1982). Managing the violent patient in the general hospital. *Postgraduate Medicine, 71*, 193-197, 200-201.

Bachrach, L. L. (1980). Is the least restrictive environment always the best? Sociological and semantic implications. *Hospital & Community Psychiatry, 31*, 97-103.

Bach-Y-Rita, G., Lion, J. R., Climent, C. E. & Ervin, F. R. (1971). Episodic dyscontrol: A study of 130 violent patients. *American Journal of Psychiatry, 127*, 1473-1478.

Baradell, J. G. (1985). Humanistic care of the patient in seclusion. *Journal of Psychosocial Nursing and Mental Health Services, 23* (2), 9-14.

Barile, L. A. (1982). A model for teaching management of disturbed behavior. *Journal of Psychosocial Nursing and Mental Health Services, 20* (11), 9-11.

Barnard, G. W., Robbins, L., Newman, G. & Carrera, F. (1984). A study of violence within a forensic treatment facility. *Bulletin of the American Academy of Psychiatry and the Law, 12*, 339-349.

Barry, D. (1984). Pharmacotherapy in violent behavior. In S. Saunders, A. M. Anderson, C. A. Hart & G. M. Rubenstein (Eds.), *Violent individuals and families: A handbook for practitioners* (pp. 226-242). Springfield, IL: Charles C Thomas.

Basque, C. O. & Merhige, J. (1980). Nurses' experiences with dangerous behavior: Implications for training. *Journal of Continuing Education in Nursing, 11* (5), 47-51.

Beier, E. G. (1966). *The silent language of psychotherapy: Social reinforcement of unconscious processes.* Chicago, IL: Aldine.

Belanger, N. & Mullen, J. K. (1984). *Safe physical management.* (Videocassette recordings and text. Available from Safe Physical Management Associates, New Bloomfield, PA.)

Bell, C. C. & Palmer, J. M. (1981). Security procedures in a psychiatric emergency service. *Journal of the National Medical Association, 73*, 835-842.

Bell, C. C. & Palmer, J. M. (1983). Survey of the demographic characteristics of patients requiring restraints in a psychiatric emergency service. *Journal of the National Medical Association, 75*, 981-987.

Benezech, M., Bourgeois, M. & Yesavage, J. (1980). Violence in the mentally ill: A study of 547 patients at a French hospital for the crimially insane. *Journal of Nervous and Mental Disease, 168*, 698-700.

Benjamin, L. S. (1982). Use of Structural Analysis of Social Behavior (SASB) to guide intervention in psychotherapy. In J. C. Anchin & D. J. Kiesler (Eds.), *Handbook of interpersonal psychotherapy* (pp. 190-212). New York: Pergamon.

Beran, N. J. & Hotz, A. M. (1984). The behavior of mentally disordered criminals in civil mental hospitals. *Hospital & Community Psychiatry, 35*, 585-589.

Bernstein, H. A. (1981). Survey of threats and assaults directed toward psychotherapists. *American Journal of Psychotherapy, 35*, 542-549.

Betancourt, A. M. & Albott, W. L. (1979). MMPI discrimination between violent and nonviolent state hospital adult male patients. *Journal of Psychiatry and Law, 7* (2), 199-209.

Bidna, H. (1975). Effects of increased security on prison violence. *Journal of Criminal Justice, 3*, 33-46.

Binder, R. L. (1979). The use of seclusion on an inpatient crisis intervention unit. *Hospital & Community Psychiatry, 30*, 266-269.

Block, B. (1976). Preparing students for physical restraint. *Journal of Psychiatric Nursing and Mental Health Services, 14* (10), 9-10.

Blount, H. R. & Chandler, T. A. (1979). Relationship between childhood abuse and assaultive behavior in adolescent male psychiatric patients. *Psychological Reports, 44*, 1126.

Boettcher, E. G. (1983). Preventing violent behavior: An integrated theoretical model for nursing. *Perspectives in Psychiatric Care, 21* (2), 54-58.

Bouras, N., Trauer, T. & Watson, J. P. (1982). Ward environment and disturbed behaviour. *Psychological Medicine, 12*, 309-319.

Brailsford, D. S. & Stevenson, J. (1973). Factors related to violent and unpredictable behaviour in psychiatric hospitals. *Nursing Times* ("Occasional Papers" supplement), *69* (3), 9-11.

Broadfoot, B. (1976). *S.P.I.T.: Defensive techniques for use with aggres-*

sive behaviors. (Available from Greene Valley Developmental Center, Greeneville, TN.)

Broadfoot, B. (1978). *Wait a minute! A look at potentially dangerous situations.* (Available from Greene Valley Developmental Center, Greeneville, TN.)

Brockner, J. & Rubin, J. Z. (1985). *Entrapment in escalating conflicts: A social psychological analysis.* New York: Springer-Verlag.

Bursten, B. (1975). Using mechanical restraints on acutely disturbed psychiatric patients. *Hospital & Community Psychiatry, 26*, 757-759.

Butcher, J. N. & Maudal, G. R. (1976). Crisis intervention. In I. B. Weiner (Ed.), *Clinical methods in psychology* (pp. 591-648). New York: John Wiley & Sons.

Campbell, W. & Mawson, D. (1978). Violence in a psychiatric unit. *Journal of Advanced Nursing, 3*, 55-64.

Caplan, G. (1964). *Principles of preventive psychiatry.* New York: Basic Books.

Carney, M. W. P. & Nolan, P. A. (1979). Management of the disturbed patient. *Nursing Times, 75*, 1896-1899.

Carson, D. I. (Speaker). (1978). A systematic approach to the violent patient. In *Managing problem patients* (Audiocassette recording 7 [23]). Glendale, CA: Audio-Digest.

Carson, D. I. (1979). Violence in the hospitalized patient. *National Association of Private Psychiatric Hospitals Journal, 10* (3), 20-27.

Castledine, G. (1981). Encounters of the violent kind. *Nursing Mirror, 153* (12), 18.

Chapman, B. (1984). *Handle with care: A revolutionay approach to institutional violence.* (Available from Handle with Care Behavior Management System, Philadelphia, PA.)

Choi, H. H. (1975). *Taekwon-Do* (2nd ed.). Ontario, Canada: International Taekwon-Do Federation.

Christy-Baker, C., & Randolph, D. S. (1982). *Working with threatened/hostile clients: A source book.* (Available from Child Welfare Training Center, Tulane University, New Orleans, LA.)

Climent, C. E. & Ervin, F. R. (1972). Historical data in the evaluation of violent patients: A hypothesis generating study. *Archives of General Psychiatry, 27*, 621-624.

Cline, F. (1980). The rageful patient. *Nurse Practitioner, 5*, 52, 54.

Cobb, J. P., & Gossop, M. R. (1976). Locked doors in the management of disturbed psychiatric patients. *Journal of Advanced Nursing, 1*, 469-480.

Coffey, M. P. (1976). The violent patient. *Journal of Advanced Nursing, 1*, 341-350.

Cohen, R. J. (1979). *Malpractice: A guide for mental health professionals.* New York: Free Press.

Confederation of Health Service Employees. (1977). *COHSE: The management of violent or potentially violent patients: Report of a special working party offering information, advice and guidance to COHSE members.* Banstead, Surrey, England: Confederation of Health Service Employees.

Confederation of Health Service Employees. (1979). *COHSE: NHS secure treatment units—a policy statement: Report of a special working party offering information, advice and guidance to COHSE members.* Banstead, Surrey, England: Confederation of Health Service Employees.

Conn, L. M. & Lion, J. R. (1983). Assaults in a university hospital. In J. R. Lion & W. H. Reid (Eds.), *Assaults within psychiatric facilities* (pp. 61-69). New York: Grune & Stratton.

Conn, L. M. & Lion, J. R. (1984). Pharmacologic approaches to violence. *Psychiatric Clinics of North America, 7*, 879-886.

Convertino, K., Pinto, R. P. & Fiester, A. R. (1980). Use of inpatient seclusion at a community mental health center. *Hospital & Community Psychiatry, 31*, 848-850.

Cooper, S. J., Browne, F. W. A., McClean, K. J. & King, D. J. (1983). Aggressive behaviour in a psychiatric observation ward. *Acta Psychiatrica Scandinavica, 68*, 386-393.

Cornfield, R. B. & Fielding, S. D. (1980). Impact of the threatening patient on ward communications. *American Journal of Psychiatry, 137*, 616-619.

Covert, A. B., Rodrigues, T. & Solomon, K. (1977). The use of mechanical and chemical restraints in nursing homes. *Journal of the American Geriatrics Society, 25* (2), 85-89.

Crabtree, L. H. (1982). Hospitalized adolescents who act out: A treatment approach. *Psychiatry, 45*, 147-158.

Craig, T. J. (1982). An epidemiologic study of problems associated with violence among psychiatric inpatients. *American Journal of Psychiatry, 139*, 1262-1266.

Crain, P. M. & Jordan, E. G. (1979). The psychiatric intensive care unit: An in-hospital treatment of violent adult patients. *Bulletin of the American Academy of Psychiatry and the Law, 9,* 190-198.

Creighton, H. (1976). Abuse of patients. *Supervisor Nurse, 7* (6), 14-15.

Creighton, H. (1978). Liability for falsifying records. *Supervisor Nurse, 9* (9), 16-17.

Creighton, H. (1979a). Standards of care. *Supervisor Nurse, 10* (3), 69-70, 73.

Creighton, H. (1979b). Incident reports—Part I. *Supervisor Nurse, 10* (10), 58-59.

Creighton, H. (1979c). Incident reports—Part II. *Supervisor Nurse, 10* (11), 79-80.

Creighton, H. (1981). Rights of mental patients. *Supervisor Nurse, 12* (5), 16-17.

Creighton, H. (1982). Unruly patients. *Nursing Management, 13* (7), 15-16.

Crowell, R. M., Tew, J. M. & Mark, V. H. (1973). Aggressive dementia associated with normal pressure hydrocephalus: Report of two unusual cases. *Neurology, 23,* 461-464.

Curran, S. F., Blatchley, R. J. & Hanlon, T. E. (1978). The relationship between body buffer zone and violence as assessed by subjective and objective techniques. *Criminal Justice and Behavior, 5* (1), 53-62.

Damijonaitis, V. (1978). A six-month study of incidents involving patients at a state psychiatric center. *Hospital & Community Psychiatry, 29,* 570-571.

Danto, B. L. (1975). Psychiatric treatment of violent patients in private practice. *International Journal of Offender Therapy and Comparative Criminology, 19* (1), 67-74.

Danto, B. L. (1982-1983). Patients who murder their psychiatrists. *American Journal of Forensic Psychiatry, 3* (3), 120-134.

Davidson, N. A., Hemingway, M. J. & Wysocki, T. (1984). Reducing the use of restrictive procedures in a residential facility. *Hospital & Community Psychiatry, 35,* 164-167.

Davis, C., Glick, I. D. & Rosow, I. (1979). The architectural design of a psychotherapeutic milieu. *Hospital & Community Psychiatry, 30,* 453-460.

Davis, E. (Speaker). (1985). Rapid tranquilization. In *Assaultive patients* (Audiocassette recording *14* [7]). Glendale, CA: Audio-Digest.

De Felippo, A. M. (1976). Preventing assaultive behavior on a psychiatric unit. *Supervisor Nurse, 7,* (6), 62-65.

Delgado-Escueta, A. V., Mattson, R. H., King, L., Goldensohn, E. S., Spiegel, H. S., Madsen, J., Crandall, P., Dreifuss, F. & Porter, R. J. (1981). The nature of aggression during epileptic seizures. *New England Journal of Medicine, 305,* 711-716.

Depp, F. C. (1976). Violent behavior patterns on psychiatric wards. *Aggressive Behavior, 2,* 295-306.

Depp, F. C. (1983). Assaults in a public mental hospital. In J. R. Lion & W. H. Reid (Eds.), *Assaults within psychiatric facilities* (pp. 21-45). New York: Grune & Stratton.

Dewhurst, K. (1970a). Nursing restraints—Past and present 1. *Nursing Times, 66,* 709-711.

Dewhurst, K. (1970b). Nursing restraints—Past and present 2: The new methods of restraint. *Nursing Times, 66,* 749-751.

Di Bella, G. A. W. (1979). Educating staff to manage threatening paranoid patients. *American Journal of Psychiatry, 136,* 333-335.

Dietz, P. E. (1981). Threats or blows? Observations on the distinction between assault and battery. *International Journal of Law and Psychiatry, 4,* 401-416.

Dietz, P. E. & Rada, R. T. (1982a). Battery incidents and batterers in a maximum security hospital. *Archives of General Psychiatry, 39,* 31-34.

Dietz, P. E. & Rada, R. T. (1982b). Risks and benefits of working with violent patients. *Psychiatric Annals, 12,* 502-508.

Dietz, P. E. & Rada, R. T. (1983a). Interpersonal violence in forensic facilities. In J. R. Lion & W. H. Reid (Eds.), *Assaults within psychiatric facilities* (pp. 47-59). New York: Grune & Stratton.

Dietz, P. E. & Rada, R. T. (1983b). Seclusion rates and patient census in a maximum security hospital. *Behavioral Sciences & The Law, 1* (4), 89-93.

DiFabio, S. (1981). Nurses' reactions to restraining patients. *American Journal of Nursing, 81,* 973-975.

DiFabio, S. & Ackerhalt, E. J. (1978). Teaching the use of restraint through role play. *Perspectives in Psychiatric Care, 16,* 218-222.

Dix, G. E. (in press). Legal and ethical issues in the treatment and handling of violent behavior. In L. Roth (Ed.), *Clinical treatment and management of the violent person.* Rockville, MD: Center for Studies of Crime and Delinquency, National Institutes of Health.

Doms, R. W., Sr. (1984). Personal distress devices for health care personnel. In J. T. Turner (Ed.), *Violence in the medical care setting: A survival guide* (pp. 225-229). Rockville, MD: Aspen.

Donlon, P. T., Hopkin, J. & Tupin, J. P. (1979). Overview: Efficacy and safety of the rapid neuroleptization method with injectable haloperidol. *American Journal of Psychiatry, 136,* 273-278.

Donlon, P. T. & Tupin, J. P. (1974). Rapid "digitalization" of decompensated schizophrenic patients with antipsychotic agents. *American Journal of Psychiatry, 131,* 310-312.

Dubin, W. R. (1981). Evaluating and managing the violent patient. *Annals of Emergency Medicine, 10,* 481-484.

Dubin, W. R. (1984). Assessment and management of psychiatric manifestations of organic brain disease. In W. R. Dubin, N. Hanke & H. W. Nickens (Eds.), *Psychiatric emergencies* (pp. 21-33). New York: Churchill Livingstone.

Dubin, W. R., Hanke, N. & Nickens, H. W. (Eds.). (1984). *Psychiatric emergencies.* New York: Churchill Livingstone.

Dubin, W. R. & Lurie, H. J. (1983). *Management and treatment of the violent patient: A video learning package.* (Videocassette recording and text. Available from IEA Productions, Inc., New York, NY.)

Dubin, W. R. & Stolberg, R. (1981). *Emergency psychiatry for the house officer.* Jamaica, NY: Spectrum.

Dyer, W. O., Murrell, D. S. & Wright, D. (1984). Training for hospital security: An alternative to training negligence lawsuits. In J. Turner (Ed.), *Violence in the medical care setting: A survival guide* (pp. 1-19). Rockville, MD: Aspen.

Edelman, S. E. (1978). Managing the violent patient in a community mental health center. *Hospital & Community Psychiatry, 29,* 460-462.

Edwards, J. G. & Reid, W. H. (1983). Violence in psychiatric facilities in Europe and the United States. In J. R. Lion & W. H. Reid (Eds.), *Assaults within psychiatric facilities* (pp. 131-142). New York: Grune & Stratton.

Edwards, K. (1978). The environment in practice. *The Practitioner, 221,* 465, 467, 469.

Edwards, K. (1979). The environment inside the hospital. *The Practitioner, 222,* 746-749, 751.

Eichelman, B. (1984). A behavioral emergency plan. *Hospital & Community Psychiatry, 35,* 1078.

Ekblom, B. (1970). *Acts of violence by patients in mental hospitals.* Uppsala, Sweden: Almqvist & Wiksells Boktryckeri AB.

Ekman, P. & Friesen, W. V. (1975). *Unmasking the face: A guide to recognizing emotions from facial clues.* Englewood Cliffs, NJ: Prentice-Hall.

Elder, J. P., Edelstein, B. A. & Narick, M. M. (1979). Adolescent psychiatric patients: Modifying aggressive behavior with social skills training. *Behavior Modification, 3* (2), 161-178.

Elgin, S. H. (1980). *The gentle art of verbal self-defense.* Englewood Cliffs, NJ: Prentice-Hall.

Ellman, J. P. (Speaker). (1984). Principles of emergency management. In *Violent patients in the emergency room* (Audiocassette recording *13* [18]). Glendale, CA: Audio-Digest.

Ennis, B. & Siegel, L. (1973). *The rights of mental patients: The basic ACLU guide to a mental patient's rights.* New York: Avon.

Ericksen, S. E., Hurt, S. W. & Davis, J. M. (1976). Dosage of antipsychotic drugs (cont.). *New England Journal of Medicine, 294,* 1296-1297.

Ernst, K. (1975). Tätlichkeiten psychiatrischer klinikpatienten in der erinnerung des pflegepersonals: Eine retrospektive erhebung. [A nursing staff's memory of aggression by psychiatric clinic patients.] *Psychiatria Clinica, 8* (4), 189-200.

Evenson, R. C., Sletten, I. W., Altman, H. & Brown, M. L. (1974). Disturbing behavior: A study of incident reports. *Psychiatric Quarterly, 48,* 266-275.

Fauman, B. J. & Fauman, M. A. (1981). *Emergency psychiatry for the house officer.* Baltimore: Williams & Wilkins.

Favell, J. E., McGimsey, J. F. & Jones, M. L. (1978). The use of restraint in the treatment of self-injury and as positive reinforcement. *Journal of Applied Behavior Analysis, 11,* 225-241.

Favell, J. E., McGimsey, J. F., Jones, M. L. & Cannon, P. R. (1981). Physical restraint as positive reinforcement. *American Journal of Mental Deficiency, 85,* 425-432.

Fein, B. A., Gareri, E. & Hansen, P. (1981). Teaching staff to cope with patient violence. *Journal of Continuing Education in Nursing, 12* (3), 7-11.

Felthous, A. R. (1984). Preventing assaults on a psychiatric inpatient ward. *Hospital & Community Psychiatry, 35,* 1223-1226.

Fitzgerald, R. G. & Long, I. (1973). Seclusion in the treatment and management of severely disturbed manic and depressed patients. *Perspectives in Psychiatric Care, 11* (2), 59-64.

Fixsen, D. L., Phillips, E. L., Dowd, T. P. & Palma, L. J. (1981). Preventing violence in residential treatment programs for adolescents. In R. B. Stuart (Ed.), *Violent behavior: Social learning approaches to prediction, management and treatment* (pp. 203-226). New York: Brunner/Mazel.

Flannelly, L., & Flannelly, K. J. (1982). Perspectives on violence from animal research. *Hospital & Community Psychiatry, 33*, 853-854.

Florida Department of Health and Rehabilitative Services. (1983). *Aggression control techniques: Instructor's guide.* (Available from State of Florida, Department of Health and Rehabilitative Services, Tallahassee, FL.)

Forquer, S. & Anderson, T. (1984). *Evaluating continuing mental health education: The development and use of a concerns-based instrument.* Unpublished manuscript, Medical College of Pennsylvania, Philadelphia.

Fottrell, E. (1980). A study of violent behaviour among patients in psychiatric hospitals. *British Journal of Psychiatry, 136*, 216-221.

Fottrell, E., Bewley, T. & Squizzoni, M. (1978). A study of aggressive and violent behaviour among a group of psychiatric in-patients. *Medicine, Science and the Law, 18*, 66-69.

Frances, A. & Weinstein, G. (1983). Dealing with the potentially violent patient who seeks help yet refuses hospitalization. *Hospital & Community Psychiatry, 34*, 679-680.

Freedman, J. (1979). Encouraging staff members to report cases of abuse. *Hospital & Community Psychiatry, 30*, 636.

Friedman, H. J. (1969). Some problems of inpatient management with borderline patients. *American Journal of Psychiatry, 126*, 299-304.

Frost, M. (1972). Violence in psychiatric patients. *Nursing Times, 68* (24), 748-749.

Frost, M. (1975). Aggressives and natural isolates. *Nursing Times, 71* (2), 471-475.

Fuqua, P. & Wilson, J. V. (1978). *Terrorism: The executive's guide to survival.* Houston, TX: Gulf.

Gair, D. S. (1980). Limit-setting and seclusion in the psychiatric hospital. *Psychiatric Opinion, 17* (2), 15-19.

Gast, D. L. & Nelson, C. M. (1977). Legal and ethical considerations for the use of timeout in special education settings. *Journal of Special Education, 11*, 457-467.

Gerlock, A. & Solomons, H. C. (1983). Factors associated with the seclusion of psychiatric patients. *Perspectives in Psychiatric Care, 21* (2), 47-53.

Gertz, B. (1980). Training for prevention of assaultive behavior in a psychiatric setting. *Hospital & Community Psychiatry, 31*, 628-630.

Glick, R. A., Meyerson, A. T., Robbins, E. & Talbott, J. A. (Eds.). (1976). *Psychiatric emergencies.* New York: Grune & Stratton.

Gosnold, J. K. (1978). The violent patient in the accident and emergency department. *Royal Society of Health Journal, 98* (4), 189-190, 198.

Greenblatt, M. (1980). Seclusion as a means of restraint. *Psychiatric Opinion, 17* (2), 13-14, 39.

Griffin, J. B., Conner, W. C., Tait, C. D. & Warren, C. D. (1968). "Tranquilizer gun" for violent persons? *Crime and Delinquency, 14*, 216-219.

Griffitt, W. & Veitch, R. (1971). Hot and crowded: Influences of population density and temperature on interpersonal affective behavior. *Journal of Personality and Social Psychology, 17*, 92-98.

Gudjonsson, G. H. & Roberts, J. C. (1981a). The aggressive behaviour of personality disordered patients and its relation to personality and perceptual motor performance. *Current Psychological Research, 1* (2), 101-109.

Gudjonsson, G. H. & Roberts, J. C. (1981b). Trail making scores as a prediction of aggressive behaviour in personality-disordered patients. *Perceptual and Motor Skills, 52*, 413-414.

Guggenheim, F. G. & Weiner, M. F. (Eds.). (1984). *Manual of psychiatric consultation and emergency care.* New York: Jason Aronson.

Guirguis, E. F. (1978). Management of disturbed patients: An alternative to the use of mechanical restraints. *Journal of Clinical Psychiatry, 39*, 295-303.

Guirguis, E. F. & Durost, H. B. (1978). The role of mechanical restraints in the management of disturbed behaviour. *Canadian Psychiatric Association Journal, 23*, 209-218.

Gutheil, T. G. (1978). Observations on the theoretical bases for seclusion of the psychiatric inpatient. *American Journal of Psychiatry, 135*, 325-328.

Gutheil, T. G. (1980). Restraint versus treatment: Seclusion as discussed in the Boston State Hospital case. *American Journal of Psychiatry, 137*, 718-719.

Gutheil, T. G. (1984). Review of individual quantitative studies. In K. Tardiff (Ed.), *The psychiatric uses of seclusion and restraint* (pp. 125-140). Washington, DC: American Psychiatric Press.

Gutheil, T. G. (1985). Prosecuting patients [letter to the editor]. *Hospital & Community Psychiatry, 36,* 1320-1321.

Gutheil, T. G., Appelbaum, P. S. & Wexler, D. B. (1983). The inappropriateness of "least restrictive alternative" analysis for involuntary procedures with the institutionalized mentally ill. *Journal of Psychiatry & Law, 11,* 7-17.

Gutheil, T. G. & Rivinus, T. M. (1982). The cost of window breaking. *Psychiatric Annals, 12* (5), 47-51.

Gutheil, T. G. & Tardiff, K. (1984). Indications and contraindications for seclusion and restraint. In K. Tardiff (Ed.), *Psychiatric uses of seclusion and restraint* (pp. 11-17). Washington, DC: American Psychiatric Press.

Haffke, E. A. & Reid, W. H. (1983). Violence against mental health personnel in Nebraska. In J. R. Lion & W. H. Reid (Eds.), *Assaults within psychiatric facilities* (pp. 91-102). New York: Grune & Stratton.

Hagen, D. Q., Mikolajczak, J. & Wright, R. (1972). Aggression in psychiatric patients. *Comprehensive Psychiatry, 13,* 481-487.

Haley, J. (1973). *Uncommon therapy: The psychiatric techniques of Milton H. Erickson, M.D.* New York: W. W. Norton.

Hall, H. V. (1982). Dangerousness predictions and the maligned forensic professional: Suggestions for detecting distortion of true basal violence. *Criminal Justice and Behavior, 9* (1), 3-12.

Hamilton, J. R. & Freeman, H. (Eds.). (1982). *Dangerousness: Psychiatric assessment and management.* London: Gaskell (The Royal College of Psychiatrists).

Hare-Mustin, R. T., Maracek, J., Kaplan, A. G. & Liss-Levenson, N. (1979). Rights of clients, responsibilities of therapists. *American Psychologist, 34,* 3-16.

Harper, R. G., Wiens, A. N. & Matarazzo, J. D. (1978). *Nonverbal communication: The state of the art.* New York: John Wiley & Sons.

Harry, B. (1983). Movies and behavior among hospitalized mentally disordered offenders. *Bulletin of the American Academy of Psychiatry and the Law, 11,* 359-364.

Hart, C. A., Broad, J. & Trimborn, S. (1984). *Managing violence in an inpatient setting.* In S. Saunders, A. M. Anderson, C. A. Hart & C. M. Rubenstein (Eds.), *Violent individuals and families: A handbook for practitioners* (pp. 164-197). Springfield, IL: Charles C Thomas.

Hartocollis, P. (1972). Aggressive behavior and the fear of violence. *Adolescence, 7,* 479-490.

Harvey, R. C. & Schepers, J. (1977). Physical control techniques and defensive holds for use with aggressive retarded adults. *Mental Retardation, 15* (5), 29-31.

Hatti, S., Dubin, W. R. & Weiss, K. J. (1982). A study of circumstances surrounding patient assaults on psychiatrists. *Hospital & Community Psychiatry, 33,* 660-661.

Havens, L. (1980). Explorations in the uses of language in psychotherapy: Counterprojective statements. *Contemporary Psychoanalysis, 16,* 53-67.

Hay, D. & Cromwell, R. (1980). Reducing the use of full-leather restraints on an acute adult inpatient ward. *Hospital & Community Psychiatry, 31,* 198-200.

Hays, J. R., Roberts, T. K. & Solway, K. S. (Eds.). (1981). *Violence and the violent individual.* New York: Spectrum.

Hellman, D. S. & Blackman, N. (1966). Enuresis, firesetting and cruelty to animals: A triad predictive of adult crime. *American Journal of Psychiatry, 122,* 1431-1435.

Heslin, R. & Patterson, M. L. (1982). *Nonverbal behavior and social psychology.* New York: Plenum.

Hildreth, A. M., Derogatis, L. R. & McCusker, K. (1971). Body buffer zone and violence: A reassessment and confirmation. *American Journal of Psychiatry, 127,* 1641-1645.

Himelstein, P. & Von Grunau, G. (1981). Differentiation of aggressive and nonaggressive schizophrenics with the hand test: Another failure. *Psychological Reports, 49,* 556.

Horowitz, M. J., Duff, D. F. & Stratton, L. O. (1964). Body-buffer zone. *Archives of General Psychiatry, 11,* 651-656.

Ilfeld, F. W. (1969). Overview of the causes and prevention of violence. *Archives of General Psychiatry, 20,* 675-689.

Infantino, J. A. & Musingo, S. Y. (1985). Assaults and injuries among staff with and without training in Aggression Control Techniques. *Hospital & Community Psychiatry, 36,* 1312-1314.

Ionno, J. A. (1983). A prospective study of assaultive behavior in female psychiatric patients. In J. R. Lion & W. H. Reid (Eds.), *As-*

saults within psychiatric facilities (pp. 71-80). New York: Grune & Stratton.

Jacobs, A. N., Brotz, C. A. & Gamel, N. N. (1973). *Critical behaviors in psychiatric-mental health nursing: Vol. II: Behavior of nurses.* Palo Alto, CA: American Institutes for Research.

Jacobs, D. (1983). Evaluation and management of the violent patient in emergency settings. *Psychiatric Clinics of North America, 6,* 259-269.

Johnston, R. & Lundy, B. W. (1982). Disruptive behavior by hospitalized patients following movie viewing. *Hospital & Community Psychiatry, 33,* 1015-1017.

Jones, M. K. (1985). Patient violence: Report of 200 incidents. *Journal of Psychosocial Nursing and Mental Health Services, 23* (6), 12-17.

Joy, D. S. (1981). The maintenance of order on an adolescent inpatient unit: An analysis of the evening shift. *Psychiatry, 44,* 253–261.

Julavits, W. F. (1983). Legal issues in emergency psychiatry. *Psychiatric Clinics of North America, 6,* 335-345.

Kalogerakis, M. G. (1971). The assaultive psychiatric patient. *Psychiatric Quarterly, 45,* 372-381.

Karshmer, J. F. (1978). The application of social learning theory to aggression. *Perspectives in Psychiatric Care, 16,* 223-227.

Katch, F. I. & McArdle, W. D. (1977). *Nutrition, weight control and exercise.* Boston: Houghton-Mifflin.

Keckich, W. A. (1978). Violence as a manifestation of akathisia. *Journal of the American Medical Association, 240,* 2185.

Kee, H. (1978). *Tang Soo Do* (Soo Bahk Do). Springfield, NJ: U. S. Tang Soo Do Moo Duk Kwan Federation.

Kermani, E. J. (1981). Violent patients: A study. *American Journal of Psychotherapy, 35* (2), 215-225.

Kilgalen, R. K. (1977). The effective use of seclusion. *Journal of Psychiatric Nursing and Mental Health Services, 15* (1), 22-25.

Killebrew, J. A., Harris, C. & Kruckeberg, K. (1982). A conceptual model for determining the least restrictive treatment-training modality. *Hospital & Community Psychiatry, 33,* 367-370.

Kinzel, A. F. (1974). Abnormalities of personal space in violent prisoners. In J. H. Cullen (Ed.), *Experimental behaviour: A basis for the study of mental disturbance* (pp. 224-229). New York: John Wiley & Sons.

Kinzel, A. F. (1979). Body-buffer zone in violent prisoners. *American Journal of Psychiatry, 127,* 59-64.

Kittel, G. (1965). *Theological dictionary of the New Testament* (Vol. 3). Grand Rapids, MI: Wm. B. Eerdmans.

Kloss, J. D. (1980). Restrictiveness: Defining its multiple dimensions. *Hospital & Community Psychiatry, 31,* 422.

Knoff, W. F. (1960). Modern treatment of the "insane": An historical overview of nonrestraint. *New York State Journal of Medicine, 60,* 2236-2243.

Kroll, J. & Mackenzie, T. B. (1983). When psychiatrists are liable: Risk managment and violent patients. *Hospital & Community Psychiatry, 34,* 29-37.

Kronberg, M. E. (1983). Nursing interventions in the management of the assaultive patient. In J. R. Lion & W. H. Reid (Eds.), *Assaults within psychiatric facilities* (pp. 225-240). New York: Grune & Stratton.

Kudo, K. (1967a). *Judo in action: Throwing techniques.* Tokyo, Japan: Japan Publications Trading Co.

Kudo, K. (1967b). *Judo in action: Grappling techniques.* Tokyo, Japan: Japan Publications Trading Co.

Kutzer, D. J. & Lion, J. R. (1984). The violent patient: Assessment and intervention. In S. Saunders, A. M. Anderson, C. A. Hart & G. M. Rubenstein (Eds.), *Violent individuals and families: A handbook for practitioners* (pp. 69-86). Springfield, IL: Charles C Thomas.

LaBrash, L. & Cain, J. (1984). A near-fatal assault on a psychiatric unit. *Hospital & Community Psychiatry, 35,* 168-169.

Lanza, M. L. (1983). The reactions of nursing staff to physical assault by a patient. *Hospital & Community Psychiatry, 34,* 44-47.

Lanza, M. L. (1984). A follow-up study of nurses' reactions to physical assault. *Hospital & Community Psychiatry, 35,* 492-494.

Lanza, M. L. (1985). How nurses react to assault. *Journal of Psychosocial Nursing and Mental Health Services, 23* (6), 6-11.

Lathrop, V. G. (1978). Aggression as a response. *Perspectives in Psychiatric Care, 16,* 202-205.

Lawson, W. B., Yesavage, J. A. & Werner, P. D. (1984). Race, violence, and psychopathology. *Journal of Clinical Psychiatry, 45* (7), 294-297.

Learning to manage assaultive behavior. (Spring 1979). *Innovations, 6,* 35-36.

Lee, B. (1975). *Tao of Jeet Kune Do.* Burbank, CA: Ohara.

Lee, R. G. (1979). Health and safety in hospitals. *Medicine, Science and the Law, 19* (2), 89-93.

Lehmann, L. S., Padilla, M., Clark, S. & Loucks, S. (1983). Training personnel in the prevention and management of violent behavior. *Hospital & Community Psychiatry, 34,* 40-43.

Lenefsky, B., de Palma, T. & Locicero, D. (1978). Management of violent behaviors. *Perspectives in Psychiatric Care, 16,* 212-217.

Levy, P. & Hartocollis, P. (1976). Nursing aides and patient violence. *American Journal of Psychiatry, 133,* 429-431.

Leyens, J. P., Camino, L., Parke, R. D. & Berkowitz, L. (1975). Effects of movie violence on aggression in a field setting as a function of group dominance and cohesion. *Journal of Personality and Social Psychology, 32,* 346-360.

Liabilities and litigation. (1983). *CPI National Report, 3* (2), 1-4.

Liberman, R. P., Marshall, B. D., Jr. & Burke, K. L. (1981). Drug and environmental interventions for aggressive psychiatric patients. In R. B. Stuart (Ed.), *Violent behavior: Social learning approaches to prediction, management and treatment* (pp. 227-264). New York: Brunner/Mazel.

Linden, R., Davis, J. M. & Rubinstein, J. (1982). High vs. low dose treatment with antipsychotic agents. *Psychiatric Annals, 12,* 769-771, 775, 778-781.

Lion, J. R. (1972a). *Evaluation and management of the violent patient: Guidelines in the hospital and institution.* Springfield, IL: Charles C Thomas.

Lion, J. R. (1972b). The role of depression in the treatment of aggressive personality disorders. *American Journal of Psychiatry, 129,* 347-349.

Lion, J. R. (1975a). Conceptual issues in the use of drugs for the treatment of aggression in man. *Journal of Nervous and Mental Disease, 160* (2), 76-82.

Lion, J. R. (1975b). Developing a violence clinic. In S. A. Pasternack (Ed.), *Violence and victims* (pp. 71-88). New York: Spectrum.

Lion, J. R. (1978). Are clinicians afraid to ask about violence? [letter to the editor]. *American Journal of Psychiatry, 135,* 757.

Lion, J. R. (1983a). Special aspects of psychopharmacology. In J. R. Lion & W. H. Reid (Eds.), *Assaults within psychiatric facilities* (pp. 287-296). New York: Grune & Stratton.

Lion, J. R. (1983b). The violent patient. In *The difficult patient: Detec-*

tion and treatment (Audiocassette recording). Philadelphia, PA: Smith Kline & French Laboratories.

Lion, J. R. & Bach-Y-Rita, G. (1970). Group psychotherapy with violent outpatients. *International Journal of Group Psychotherapy, 20* (2), 185-191.

Lion, J. R., Bach-Y-Rita, J. R. & Ervin, F. R. (1968). The self-referred violent patient. *Journal of the American Medical Association, 205,* 503-505.

Lion, J. R., Bach-Y-Rita, G. & Ervin, F. R. (1969). Violent patients in the emergency room. *American Journal of Psychiatry, 125,* 1706-1711.

Lion, J. R., Christopher, R. L. & Madden, D. J. (1977). A group approach with violent outpatients. *International Journal of Group Psychotherapy, 27* (1), 67-74.

Lion, J. R., Levenberg, L. B. & Strange, R. E. (1972). Restraining the violent patient. *Journal of Psychiatric Nursing and Mental Health Services, 10* (2), 9-11.

Lion, J. R., Madden, D. J. & Christopher, R. L. (1976). A violence clinic: Three years' experience. *American Journal of Psychiatry, 133,* 432-435.

Lion, J. R. & Pasternak, S. A. (1973). Countertransference reactions to violent patients. *American Journal of Psychiatry, 130,* 207-210.

Lion, J. R. & Reid, W. H. (Eds.). (1983). *Assaults within psychiatric facilities.* New York: Grune & Stratton.

Lion, J. R., Snyder, W. & Merrill, G. L. (1981). Underreporting of assaults on staff in a state hospital. *Hospital & Community Psychiatry, 32,* 497-498.

Lion, J. R. & Soloff, P. H. (1984). Implementation of seclusion and restraint. In K. Tardiff (Ed.), *Psychiatric uses of seclusion and reraint* (pp. 19-34). Washington, DC: American Psychiatric Press.

Lipp, M. & Weingarten, R. (1975). Hazards in the practice of medicine. *American Family Physician, 12* (4), 92-96.

Loomis, M. E. (1970). Nursing management of acting-out behavior. *Perspectives in Psychiatric Care, 8* (4), 168-173.

Lorenz, K. (1966). *On aggression.* New York: Harcourt, Brace & World.

Lowenstein, L. F. (1979). Physical restraints as an alternative to punishment and the maximum security confinement. *Community Home & School Gazette, 73,* 152-158.

Lyon, G. G. (1970). Limit setting as a therapeutic tool. *Journal of Psychiatric Nursing, 8* (6), 17-24.

MacVicar, K. (1978). Splitting and identification with the aggressor in assaultive borderline patients. *American Journal of Psychiatry, 135*, 229-231.

Madden, D. J. (1977). Voluntary and involuntary treatment of aggressive patients. *American Journal of Psychiatry, 134*, 553-555.

Madden, D. J. (1982). Psychotherapy with violent patients. *Psychiatric Annals, 12*, 517-521.

Madden, D. J., Lion, J. R. & Penna, M. W. (1976). Assaults on psychiatrists by patients. *American Journal of Psychiatry, 133*, 422-425.

Mark, V. H. & Ervin, F. R. (1970). *Violence and the brain.* New York: Harper & Row.

Marohn, R. C., Dalle-Molle, D., Offer, D. & Ostrov, E. (1973). A hospital riot: Its determinants and implications for treatment. *American Journal of Psychiatry, 130*, 631-636.

Mason, A. S. & Granacher, R. P. (1976). Basic principles of rapid neuroloptization. *Diseases of the Nervous System, 37*, 547-551.

Mattson, M. R. & Sacks, M. H. (1978). Seclusion: Uses and complications. *American Journal of Psychiatry, 135*, 1210-1213.

McArthur, C. H. (1972). Nursing violent patients under security restrictions. *Nursing Mirror, 68*, 861-863.

McGreevy, M. A., Steadman, H. J. & Way, B. (1984). Assessing the operation of secure care programs in New York state facilities. *Hospital & Community Psychiatry, 35*, 589-594.

McKenna, J. J. (1983). Primate aggression and evolution: An overview of sociobiological and anthropological perspectives. *Bulletin of the American Academy of Psychiatry and the Law, 11* (2), 105-130.

Med schools urged to teach self-protection (August 7, 1981). *Psychiatric News*, p. 27.

Megargee, E. I. (1970). Undercontrolled and overcontrolled personality types in extreme antisocial aggression. In E. I. Megargee & J. E. Hokanson (Eds.), *The dynamics of aggression* (pp. 108-120). New York: Harper & Row.

Megargee, E. I. (1976). The prediction of dangerous behavior. *Criminal Justice and Behavior, 3* (1), 3-22.

Megargee, E. I. (1981). Methodological problems in the prediction of violence. In J. R. Hays, T. K. Roberts & K. S. Solway (Eds.), *Violence and the violent individual* (pp. 179-191). New York: Spectrum.

Megargee, E. I. & Hokanson, J. E. (1970). *The dynamics of aggression.* New York: Harper & Row.

Mehr, J. J. & Hollerauer, T. C. (1984). Behavioral treatment for aggression in residents of institutions for the emotionally disturbed and the mentally retarded. In S. Saunders, A. M. Anderson, C. H. Hart & G. M. Rubenstein (Eds.), *Violent individuals and families: A handbook for practitioners* (pp. 198-225). Springfield, IL: Charles C Thomas.

Melbin, M. (1969). Behavior rhythms in mental hospitals. *American Journal of Sociology, 74*, 650-665.

Menzies, R. J., Webster, C. D. & Butler, B. T. (1981). Perceptions of dangerousness among forensic psychiatrists. *Comprehensive Psychiatry, 22* (4), 387-396.

Mikolajczak, J. & Hagen, D. Q. (1978). Aggression in psychiatric patients in a VA hospital. *Military Medicine, 143*, 402-405.

Miller, R. D. (1985). The harassment of forensic psychiatrists outside of court. *Bulletin of the American Academy of Psychiatry and the Law, 13*, 337-343.

Mills, M. J., Phelan, L. & Ryan, J. A. (1985). In reply [letter to the editor]. *Hospital & Community Psychiatry, 36*, 1321-1322.

Misik, I. (1981). About using restraints: With restraint. *Nursing '81, 11* (8), 50-55.

Monahan, J. (1982). Clinical prediction of violent behavior. *Psychiatric Annals, 12*, 509-513.

Monahan, J. (1984). The prediction of violent behavior: Toward a second generation of theory and policy. *American Journal of Psychiatry, 141*, 1-15.

Moore, J. A. (1968). Encountering hostility during psychotherapy sessions. *Perspectives in Psychiatric Care, 6* (2), 58-65.

Moran, J. F. (1984). Teaching the management of violent behavior to nursing staff: A health care model. In J. T. Turner (Ed.), *Violence in the medical care setting: A survival guide* (pp. 231-249). Rockville, MD: Aspen.

Mulvey, E. P. & Lidz, C. W. (1984). Clinical considerations in the prediction of dangerousness in mental patients. *Clinical Psychology Review, 4*, 379-401.

Nadelson, T. (1977). Borderline rage and the therapist's response. *American Journal of Psychiatry, 134*, 748-751.

Nations, W. C. (1973). What constitutes abuse of patients? *Hospitals, 47* (23), 51-53.

Nelson, B. (June 14, 1983). Acts of violence against therapists pose lurking threat. *New York Times*, pp. C1, C8.

New York State Office of Mental Retardation and Developmental Disabilities. (1980). *Physical intervention techniques.* (Videocassette recording and text. Available from Bureau of Staff Development and Training, New York State Office of Mental Retardation and Developmental Disabilities, Albany, NY.)

New York State Office of Mental Retardation and Developmental Disabilities. (1982). *Behavior management for the aggressive client.* (Available from Bureau of Staff Development and Training, New York State Office of Mental Retardation and Developmental Disabilities, Albany, NY.)

Nickens, H. W. (1984). Assessment and management of the violent patient. In W. R. Dubin, N. Hanke & H. W. Nickens (Eds.), *Psychiatric emergencies* (pp. 101-109). New York: Churchill Livingstone.

Nigrosh, B. J. (1983). Physical contact skills in specialized training for the prevention and management of violence. In J. R. Lion & W. H. Reid (Eds.), *Assaults within psychiatric facilities* (pp. 265-285). New York: Grune & Stratton.

Noone, J. A., Molnar, G. & Hopper-Small, C. (1979). Dislocation of expectations: Management of violence on a general hospital psychiatric unit. *Canadian Journal of Psychiatry, 24*, 213-217.

Nordlicht, S. (1972). Determinants of violence. *New York State Journal of Medicine, 72*, 2163-2165.

Northrup, G. (1982). Theory and practice of restraints part I: Before the restraint. *Milieu Therapy, 2* (1), 60-68.

Northrup, G. (1983). Theory and practice of restraints part II: The restraint and afterward. *Milieu Therapy, 3* (1), 40-53.

Ochitill, H. N. (1983). Violence in a general hospital. In J. R. Lion & W. H. Reid (Eds.), *Assaults within psychiatric facilities* (pp. 103-130). New York: Grune & Stratton.

Ochitill, H. N. & Krieger, M. (1982). Violent behavior among hospitalized medical and surgical patients. *Southern Medical Journal, 75* (2), 151-156.

Offer, D., Marohn, R. C. & Ostrow, E. (1975). Violence among hospitalized delinquents. *Archives of General Psychiatry, 32*, 1180-1186.

Okin, R. L. (1985). Variation among state hospitals in use of seclusion and restraint. *Hospital & Community Psychiatry, 36*, 648-652.

Oldham, J. M., Russakoff, L. M. & Prusnofsky, L. (1983). Seclusion: Patterns and milieu. *Journal of Nervous and Mental Disease, 171*, 645-650.

Oxford English dictionary (Vol. 2). (1933). London: Oxford University Press.

Ozarin, L. D. (1980). Notes on the development of collaboration between architects and clinicians. *Hospital & Community Psychiatry, 31*, 276-277.

Parks, S. L. (1966). Allowing physical distance as a nursing approach. *Perspectives in Psychiatric Care, 4* (6), 31-35.

Pasternack, S. A. (Ed.). (1975). *Violence and victims.* New York: Spectrum.

Patient behavior: Limits on R.N. liability. (1981). *Regan Report on Nursing Law, 22* (2).

Pellegrini, R. J., Schauss, A. G. & Miller, M. E. (1981). Room color and aggression in a criminal detention holding cell: A test of the "tranquilizing pink" hypothesis. *Orthomolecular Psychiatry, 10* (3), 174-181.

Penna, M. W. (1983). The effect of the milieu on assaults. In J. R. Lion & W. H. Reid (Eds.), *Assaults within psychiatric facilities* (pp. 297-310). New York: Grune & Stratton.

Penningroth, P. E. (1975). Control of violence in a mental health setting. *American Journal of Nursing, 75*, 606-609.

Perry, S. W. & Gilmore, M. M. (1981). The disruptive patient or visitor. *Journal of the American Medical Association, 245*, 755-757.

Petrie, W. M. (1984). Violence: The geriatric patient. In J. T. Turner (Ed.), *Violence in the medical care setting: A survival guide* (pp. 107-121). Rockville, MD: Aspen.

Petrie, W. M., Lawson, E. C. & Hollander, M. H. (1982). Violence in geriatric patients. *Journal of the American Medical Association, 248*, 443-444.

Pfeffer, C. R., Plutchik, R. & Mizruchi, M. S. (1983). Predictors of assaultiveness in latency age children. *American Journal of Psychiatry, 140*, 31-35.

Phelan, L. A., Mills, M. J. & Ryan, J. A. (1985). Prosecuting psychiatric patients for assault. *Hospital & Community Psychiatry, 36*, 581-582.

Phillips, P. & Nasr, S. J. (1983). Seclusion and restraint and prediction of violence. *American Journal of Psychiatry, 140*, 229-232.

Piercy, D. (1984). Violence: The drug/alcohol patient. In J. T. Turner (Ed.), *Violence in the medical care setting: A survival guide* (pp. 123-151). Rockville, MD: Aspen.

Pisarcik, G. (1981). Facing the violent patient. *Nursing '81, 11* (9), 62-65.

Pizer, H. (1980). Executive protection: The view from the private security sector. In R. H. Shultz, Jr. & S. Sloan (Eds.), *Responding to the terrorist threat: Security and crisis management* (pp. 105-114). New York: Pergamon.

Plutchik, R., Karasu, T. B., Conte, H. R., Siegel, B. & Jerrett, I. (1978). Toward a rationale for the seclusion process. *Journal of Nervous and Mental Disease, 166*, 571-579.

Pribula, I. P. (1977). Disarming the agitated, combative or destructive patient. *Free Association, 4* (1), 1-3.

Program for the prevention and management of disturbed behaviour. (1976). *Hospital & Community Psychiatry, 27*, 724-727.

Psychiatric emergencies. (1978). *Emergency Nurse Legal Bulletin, 4* (2), 2-8.

Psychiatric emergencies: Update. (1980). *Emergency Nurse Legal Bulletin, 6* (3), 2-10.

Psychiatric nursing: Restraint and supervision of patients. (1981). *Regan Report on Nursing Law, 22* (1).

Qadir, G. (1982). Violence in an open psychiatric unit. *Journal of Psychiatric Treatment and Evaluation, 4*, 409-413.

Quinsey, V. L. (1977a). Problems in the treatment of mentally disordered offenders. *Canada's Mental Health, 25*, 2-3.

Quinsey, V. L. (1977b). Studies in the reduction of assaults in a maximum security psychiatric institution. *Canada's Mental Health, 25*, 21-23.

Quinsey, V. L. (1979). Assessments of the dangerousness of mental patients held in maximum security. *International Journal of Law and Psychiatry, 2*, 389-406.

Quinsey, V. L. & Varney, G. W. (November 1977). Characteristics of assaults and assaulters in a maximum security psychiatric unit. *Crime and/et Justice*, 212-220.

Rabin, P. L. & Koomen, J. (1982). The violent patient: Differential diagnosis and management. *Journal of the Tennessee Medical Association, 75*, 313-317.

Rabkin, J. G. (1979). Criminal behavior of discharged mental patients: A critical appraisal of the research. *Psychological Bulletin, 86*, 1-27.

Rachlin, S. (1982). Toward a definition of staff rights. *Hospital & Community Psychiatry, 33*, 60-61.

Rada, R. T. (1981). The violent patient: Rapid assessment and management. *Psychosomatics, 22* (2), 101-109.

Ramchandani, D., Salman, A. & Helfrich, J. (1981). Seclusion of psychiatric patients: A general hospital perspective. *International Journal of Social Psychiatry, 27* (4), 309-315.

Ramirez, L. F., Bruce, J. & Whaley, M. (1981). An educational program for the prevention and management of disturbed behavior in psychiatric settings. *Journal of Continuing Education in Nursing, 12* (5), 19-21.

Rampling, D. (1978). Aggression: A paradoxical response to tricyclic antidepressants. *American Journal of Psychiatry, 135,* 117-118.

Ransohoff, P. (1980). A comment on the dimensions and context of restrictiveness. *Hospital & Community Psychiatry, 31,* 639.

Ransohoff, P., Zachary, R. A., Gaynor, J. & Hargreaves, W. A. (1982). Measuring restrictiveness of psychiatric care. *Hospital & Community Psychiatry, 33,* 361-366.

Reid, J. A. (1973). Controlling the fight/flight patient. *Canadian Nurse, 69* (10), 30-34.

Reid, W. H. (Ed.). (1981). *The treatment of antisocial syndromes.* New York: Van Nostrand Reinhold.

Reid, W. H., Bollinger, M. F. & Edwards, G. (1985). Assaults in hospitals. *Bulletin of the American Academy of Psychiatry and the Law, 13* (1), 1-4.

Reid, W. H. & Gutnik, B. D. (1982). Organic treatment of chronically violent patients. *Psychiatric Annals, 12,* 526-532.

Reinhardt, H. E. (1979). Statistical theory and clinical practice in predicting rare phenomena. *Psychological Reports, 45,* 468-470.

"Restrain as needed": Nursing judgment required. (1982). *Regan Report on Nursing Law, 23* (3).

Restraining patients in psychiatric units: Legalities. (1982). *Regan Report on Nursing Law, 23* (2).

Restraint vs. assault: R.N. legalities. (1979). *Regan Report on Nursing Law, 20* (4).

Richmond, J. S. & Ruparel, M. K. (1980). Management of violent patients in a psychiatry walk-in clinic. *Journal of Clinical Psychiatry, 41,* 370-373.

Rinn, R. C. (1976). Effects of nursing apparel upon psychiatric inpatients' behavior. *Perceptual and Motor Skills, 43,* 939-945.

Rockwell, D. A. (1972). Can you spot potential violence in a patient? *Hospital Physician, 8* (10), 52-56.

Rofman, E. S., Askinazi, C. & Fant, E. (1980). The prediction of dangerous behavior in emergency civil commitment. *American Journal of Psychiatry, 137,* 1061-1064.

Roger, D. B. & Schalekamp, E. E. (1976). Body-buffer zone and violence: A cross-cultural study. *Journal of Social Psychology, 98,* 153-158.

Rogers, R., Ciula, B. & Cavenaugh, J. L. (1980). Aggressive and socially disruptive behavior among maximum security psychiatric patients. *Psychological Reports, 46,* 291-294.

Romoff, V. I. & Kyes, J. (1979). Violence prevention. *Behavioral Issues, 1* (1).

Roper, J. M., Coutts, A., Sather, J. & Taylor, R. (1985). Restraint and seclusion: A standard and standard care plan. *Journal of Psychosocial Nursing and Mental Health Services, 23* (6), 18-23.

Rosen, H. & DiGiacomo, J. N. (1978). The role of physical restraint in the treatment of psychiatric illness. *Journal of Clinical Psychiatry, 39,* 228-232.

Rossi, D. J. (1984). From classroom to time out room: Practical and successful strategies. *CPI National Report, 4* (2), 14-15.

Roth, L. H. (Ed.). (in press). *Clinical treatment and management of the violent person.* Rockville, MD: Center for Studies of Crime and Delinquency, National Institutes of Health.

Ruben, H. L. (1981). The dangerous patient. *American Family Physician, 23* (2), 145-148.

Ruben, I., Wolkon, G. & Yamamoto, J. (1980). Physical attacks on psychiatric residents by patients. *Journal of Nervous and Mental Disease, 168,* 243-245.

Rund, D. A. & Hutzler, J. C. (1983). *Emergency psychiatry.* St. Louis: C. V. Mosby.

Sadoff, R. L. (1982). *Legal issues in the care of psychiatric patients: A guide for the mental health professional.* New York: Springer.

Sadoff, R. L. (1984). Legal issues in the care and treatment of psychiatric emergencies. In W. R. Dubin, N. Hanke & H. W. Nickens (Eds.), *Psychiatric emergencies* (pp. 233-244). New York: Churchill Livingstone.

Saito, M. (1975). *Aikido: Its heart and appearance.* Tokyo, Japan: Minato Research & Publishing.

Salamon, I. (1976). Violent and aggressive behavior. In R. A. Glick, A. T. Meyerson, E. Robbins & J. A. Talbott (Eds.), *Psychiatric emergencies* (pp. 109-119). New York: Grune & Stratton.

Sales, B. D., Overcast, T. D. & Merrikin, K. J. (1983). Worker's compensation protection for assaults and batteries on mental health professionals. In J. R. Lion & W. H. Reid (Eds.), *Assaults within psychiatric facilities* (pp. 191-210). New York: Grune & Stratton.

Salzman, C., Kochansky, G. E., Shader, R. I., Porrino, L. J., Harmatz, J. S. & Swett, C. P. (1974). Chlordiazepoxide-induced hostility in a small group setting. *Archives of General Psychiatry, 31*, 401-405.

Samuels, M. S. & Moriarty, P. H. (1979a). *One step ahead* (Videocassette recording and text). Northbrook, IL: MTI Teleprograms.

Samuels, M. S. & Moriarty, P. H. (1979b). *The seclusion room* (Videocassette recording and text). Northbrook, IL: MTI Teleprograms.

Samuels, M. S. & Moriarty, P. H. (1979c). *Verbal techniques* (Videocassette recording and text). Northbrook, IL: MTI Teleprograms.

Saposnek, D. T. (1980). Aikido: A model for brief strategic therapy. *Family Process, 19*, 227-238.

Saunders, S., Anderson, A. M., Hart, C. A. & Rubenstein, G. M. (Eds.). (1984). *Violent individuals and families: A handbook for practitioners.* Springfield, IL: Charles C Thomas.

Schoenfeld, L. S. & Lehmann, L. S. (1981). Management of the aggressive patient. In C. E. Walker (Ed.), *Clinical practice of psychology: A guide for mental health professionals* (pp. 214-243). New York: Pergamon.

Schultz, L. G. (1984). *The social service worker as victim of violence: Policy and practice implications for West Virginia.* Morgantown, WV: West Virginia University School of Social Work.

Schwab, P. J. & Lahmeyer, C. B. (1979). The uses of seclusion on a general hospital psychiatric unit. *Journal of Clinical Psychiatry, 40*, 228-231.

Schwartz, C. J. & Greenfield, G. P. (1978). Charging a patient with assault of a nurse on a psychiatric unit. *Canadian Psychiatric Association Journal, 23*, 197-200.

Serrill, M. S. (1985). Zap! Stun guns: Hot but getting heat. *Time, 125* (19), 59.

Settle, E. C. (1982). Rapid neuroleptization in a rural setting. *Psychiatric Annals, 12*, 792-795.

Settle, E. C. (1984). Rapid neuroleptization. In F. G. Guggenheim & M. F. Weiner (Eds.), *Manual of psychiatric consultation and emergency care* (pp. 43-48). New York: Jason Aronson.

Shader, R. I. (Ed.). (1975). *Manual of psychiatric therapeutics: Practical psychopharmacology and psychiatry.* Boston: Little, Brown.

Shader, R. I., Jackson, A. H., Harmatz, J. S. & Appelbaum, P. S. (1977). Patterns of violent behavior among schizophrenic inpatients. *Diseases of the Nervous System, 38*, 13-16.

Shapiro, T. (1979). *Clinical psycholinguistics.* New York: Plenum.

Sheard, M. H. (1984). Clinical pharmacology of aggressive behavior. *Clinical Neuropharmacology, 7*, 173-183.

Sheard, M. H. (Speaker). (1985). Understanding and managing violence. In *Assaultive Patients* (Audiocassette recording *14* [7]). Glendale, CA: Audio-Digest.

Shevitz, S. (1978). Emergency management of the agitated patient. *Primary Care, 5*, 625-634.

Skodol, A. E. & Karasu, T. (1978). Emergency psychiatry and the assaultive patient. *American Journal of Psychiatry, 135*, 202-205.

Slaby, A. E. (1984). Quality assurance and diagnostic psychiatry. In W. R. Dubin, N. Hanke & H. W. Nickens (Eds.), *Psychiatric emergencies* (pp. 1-20). New York: Churchill Livingstone.

Smith, B. J. & Delahaye, B. L. (1983). *How to be an effective trainer: Skills for managers and new trainers.* New York: John Wiley & Sons.

Snellgrove, C. E. & Flaherty, E. L. (1975). An attitude therapy program helps reduce the use of physical restraints. *Hospital & Community Psychiatry, 26*, 137-138.

Snyder, W., III. (1983). Administrative monitoring of assaultive patients and staff. In J. R. Lion & W. H. Reid (Eds.), *Assaults within psychiatric facilities* (pp. 157-172). New York: Grune & Stratton.

Soloff, P. H. (1978). Behavioral precipitants of restraint in the modern milieu. *Comprehensive Psychiatry, 19* (2), 179-184.

Soloff, P. H. (1979). Physical restraint and the nonpsychotic patient: Clinical and legal perspectives. *Journal of Clinical Psychiatry, 40*, 302-305.

Soloff, P. H. (1983). Seclusion and restraint. In J. R. Lion & W. H. Reid (Eds.), *Assaults within psychiatric facilities* (pp. 241-264). New York: Grune & Stratton.

Soloff, P. H. (1984). Historical notes on seclusion and restraint. In K. Tardiff (Ed.), *Psychiatric uses of seclusion and restraint* (pp. 1-9). Washington, DC: American Psychiatric Press.

Soloff, P. H. (in press). Physical controls: The role of seclusion and restraint in modern psychiatric practice. In L. H. Roth (Ed.), *Clinical treatment and management of the violent person.* Rockville, MD: Center for Studies of Crime and Delinquency, National Institutes of Health.

Soloff, P. H., Gutheil, T. G. & Wexler, D. B. (1985). Seclusion and restraint in 1985: A review and update. *Hospital & Community Psychaitry, 36*, 652-657.

Soloff, P. H. & Turner, S. M. (1981). Patterns of seclusion: A prospective study. *Journal of Nervous and Mental Disease, 169*, 37-44.

Spellacy, F. (1977). Neurolopsychological differences between violent and nonviolent adolescents. *Journal of Clinical Psychology, 33*, 966-969.

Staffs said to need training in managing violent patients. (August 7, 1981). *Psychiatric News*, pp. 26-27.

Star, B. (1984). Patient violence/therapist safety. *Social Work, 29*, 225-230.

Steadman, H. J. (1983). The risky professions. *Hospital & Community Psychiatry, 34*, 5.

Steadman, H. J. & Cocozza, J. (1978). Psychiatry, dangerousness and the repetitively violent offender. *Journal of Criminal Law & Criminology, 69* (2), 226-231.

Stegne, L. R. (1975). *The prevention and management of disturbed behaviour* (Videocassette recording and text. Available from Ontario Government Bookstore, Toronto, Ontario).

Steiger, L. K. (1985). What is Baker-Miller pink? *CPI National Report, 4* (4), 1, 3-4.

Stein, L. I. & Diamond, R. J. (1985). The chronic mentally ill and the criminal justice system: When to call the police. *Hospital & Community Psychiatry, 36*, 271-274.

Stewart, A. T. (1978). Handling the aggressive patient. *Perspectives in Psychiatric Care, 16*, 228-232.

Stokman, C. L. J. (1982). Violence among hospitalized patients. *Hospital & Community Psychiatry, 33*, 986.

Stokman, C. L. J. & Heiber, P. (1982). Incidents in hospitalized forensic patients. *Victimology: An International Journal, 5*, 175-192.

Stone, A. A. (1984). The new paradox of psychiatric malpractice. *New England Journal of Medicine, 311*, 1384-1387.

Straker, M., Carman, P., Fulton, J. & Smith, M. (1977). Assaultive behaviors in an institutional setting. *Psychiatric Journal of the University of Ottawa, 2*, 185-190.

Strentz, T. (1984). Hostage survival guidelines. In J. T. Turner (Ed.), *Violence in the medical care setting: A survival guide* (pp. 183-208). Rockville, MD: Aspen.

Strupp, H. H. & Binder, J. L. (1984). *Psychotherapy in a new key: A guide to time-limited dynamic psychotherapy*. New York: Basic Books.

Stuart, R. B. (Ed). (1981). *Violent behavior: Approaches to prediction, management and treatment*. New York: Brunner/Mazel.

Sundram, C. J. (1984). Obstacles to reducing patient abuse in public institutions. *Hospital & Community Psychiatry, 35*, 238-243.

Switzky, H. N. & Miller, T. L. (1978). The least restrictive alternative. *Mental Retardation, 16*, 52-54.

Synthesis Communications. (1981). *Management of violent patients* (Audiocassette recording and text. Available from Pfizer Pharmaceuticals, New York, NY).

Taitz, S. (Ed.). (1984). *The health care security crisis handbook: How to prevent, deal with, and reduce liability from violence and violent crime in hospitals and nursing homes*. Port Washington, NY: Rusting.

Tardiff, K. (1974). A survey of psychiatrists in Boston and their work with violent patients. *American Journal of Psychiatry, 131*, 1008-1011.

Tardiff, K. (1981a). Assault in hospitals and placement in the community. *Bulletin of the American Academy of Psychiatry and the Law, 9*, 33-39.

Tardiff, K. (1981b). Emergency control measures for psychiatric inpatients. *Journal of Nervous and Mental Disease, 169*, 614-618.

Tardiff, K. (1981c). The risk of assaultive behavior in suicidal patients: II. An inpatient survey. *Acta Psychiatrica Scandinavica, 64*, 295-300.

Tardiff, K. (1982a). A survey of five types of dangerous behavior among chronic psychiatric patients. *Bulletin of the American Academy of Psychiatry and the Law, 10*, 177-182.

Tardiff, K. (1982b). Violence in geriatric patients. *Journal of the American Medical Association, 248*, 471.

Tardiff, K. (1983a). A survey of assault by chronic patients in a state hospital system. In J. R. Lion & W. H. Reid (Eds.), *Assaults within psychiatric facilities* (pp. 3-19). New York: Grune & Stratton.

Tardiff, K. (1983b). A survey of drugs used in the management of assaultive inpatients. *Bulletin of the American Academy of Psychiatry and the Law, 11*, 215-222.

Tardiff, K. (1984a). Characteristics of assaultive patients in private hospitals. *American Journal of Psychiatry, 141*, 1232-1235.

Tardiff, K. (Ed.). (1984b). *The psychiatric uses of seclusion and restraint*. Washington, DC: American Psychiatric Press.

Tardiff, K. (1984c). Violence: The psychiatric patient. In J. Turner (Ed.), *Violence in the medical setting: A survival guide* (pp. 33-55). Rockville, MD: Aspen.

Tardiff, K. (1984d). The violent patient. In F. G. Guggenheim & M. F. Weiner (Eds.), *Manual of psychiatric consultation and emergency care* (pp. 15-22). New York: Jason Aronson.

Tardiff, K. & Deane, K. (1980). The psychological and physical status of chronic psychiatric inpatients. *Comprehensive Psychiatry, 21* (1), 91-97.

Tardiff, K. & Mattson, M. R. (1984). A survey of state mental health directors concerning guidelines for seclusion and restraint. In K. Tardiff (Ed.), *Psychiatric uses of seclusion and restraint* (pp. 141-150). Washington, DC: American Psychiatric Press.

Tardiff, K. & Maurice, W. L. (1977). The care of violent patients by psychiatrists: A tale of two cities. *Canadian Psychiatric Association Journal, 22,* 83-86.

Tardiff, K. & Sweillam, A. (1979). The relation of age to assaultive behavior in mental patients. *Hospital & Community Psychiatry, 30,* 709-711.

Tardiff, K. & Sweillam, A. (1980a). Assault, suicide and mental illness. *Archives of General Psychiatry, 37,* 164-169.

Tardiff, K. & Sweillam, A. (1980b). Factors related to increased risk of assaultive behavior in suicidal patients. *Acta Psychiatrica Scandinavica, 62,* 63-68.

Tardiff, K. & Sweillam, A. (1982). Assaultive behavior among chronic inpatients. *American Journal of Psychiatry, 139,* 212-215.

Telintelo, S., Kuhlman, T. L. & Winget, C. (1983). A study of the use of restraint in a psychiatric emergency room. *Hospital & Community Psychiatry, 34,* 164-165.

Texas Department of Mental Health and Mental Retardation. (1982a). *Prevention and management of aggressive behaviors: Introduction* (Videocassette recording. Available from Rusk State Hospital, Rusk, TX).

Texas Department of Mental Health and Mental Retardation. (1982b). *Prevention and management of aggressive behaviors: Protection of self and others* (Videocassette recording. Available from Rusk State Hospital, Rusk, TX).

Texas Department of Mental Health and Mental Retardation. (1982c). *Prevention and management of aggressive behaviors: Methods of restraint and seclusion* (Videocassette recording. Available from Rusk State Hospital, Rusk, TX).

Texas Department of Mental Health and Mental Retardation. (1982d). *Prevention and management of aggressive behaviors: Recovery of objects* (Videocassette recording. Available from Rusk State Hospital, Rusk, TX).

Texas Department of Mental Health requires employee training in the prevention and management of aggressive behavior. (June 12, 1984). *NASMHPD State Report*. Washington, DC: National Association of State Mental Health Program Directors.

Thackrey, M. (1982). Behavior: Selfness/circumjacence and nomothetic idiography (Doctoral dissertation, Vanderbilt University). *Dissertation Abstracts International, 43*, 1243B.

Thackrey, M. (1985). An outpatient P.R.N. clinic. *Hospital & Community Psychiatry, 36*, 572.

Thackrey, M. (1986). *Psychological/physical crisis intervention: Therapeutics for aggression* (Videocassette recording and text. Available from author, P.O. Box 8047, Gallatin, TN 37066).

Thackrey, M. (in press). Clinician confidence in coping with patient aggression: Assessment and enhancement. *Professional Psychology*.

Tuason, V. B. (1971). The psychiatrist and the violent patient. *Diseases of the Nervous System, 32*, 764-768.

Tupin, J. P. (1975). Management of violent patients. In R. I. Shader (Ed.), *Manual of psychiatric therapeutics: Practical psychopharmacology and psychiatry* (pp. 125-136). Boston: Little, Brown.

Tupin, J. P. (Speaker). (1978). Management strategies. In *The violent patient: Assessment and management* (Audiocassette recording 7 [8]). Glendale, CA: Audio-Digest.

Tupin, J. P. (1983). The violent patient: A strategy for management and diagnosis. *Hospital & Community Psychiatry, 34*, 37-40.

Turner, J. T. (1984a). Hostage incidents in health care settings. In J. T. Turner (Ed.), *Violence in the medical care setting: A survival guide* (pp. 171-181). Rockville, MD: Aspen.

Turner, J. T. (1984b). Role of the ED nurse in health care-based hostage incidents. *Journal of Emergency Nursing, 10*, 190-193.

Turner, J. T. (Ed.). (1984c). *Violence in the medical care setting: A survival guide*. Rockville, MD: Aspen.

Turner, J. T. (1985). Writing an organizational response plan: Hostage-taking incidents. *Journal of Healthcare Protection Management, 1* (2), 110-114.

Turns, D. M. & Gruenberg, E. M. (1973). An attendant is murdered: The state hospital responds. *Psychiatric Quarterly, 47*, 487-494.

Understanding hostility: Programmed instruction. (1967). *American Journal of Nursing, 67*, 2131-2150.

Upchurch, T. T., Ham, L., Daniels, R., McGhee, M. R. & Burnett, M. (1980). *A better way: An illustrated guide to Preventive Intervention Techniques.* (Available from Murdoch Center, Butner, NC.)

Van Hoose, W. H. & Kottler, J. A. (1985). *Ethical and legal issues in counseling and psychotherapy: A comprehensive guide* (2nd ed.). San Francisco, CA: Jossey-Bass.

Veterans Administration, Department of Medicine and Surgery, Mental Health and Behavioral Sciences Service (1978). *Management of the violent and suicidal patient* (Program Guide G-15, M-2, Part X). Washington, DC: Veterans Administration.

Violence against nurses. (1972). *British Medical Journal 4,* 129-130.

Wadeson, H. & Carpenter, W. T., Jr. (1976). Impact of the seclusion room experience. *Journal of Nervous and Mental Disease, 163*, 319-328.

Walker, C. E. (Ed.). (1981). *Clinical practice of psychology: A guide for mental health professionals.* New York: Pergamon.

Walker, E. A. (1970). Egaz moniz. In W. Haymaker & F. Schiller (Eds.), *Founders of neurology: One hundred forty-six biographical sketches by eighty-eight authors* (2nd ed.) (pp. 489-492). Springfield, IL: Charles C Thomas.

Walker, J. I. (1983). *Psychiatric emergencies: Intervention and resolution.* Philadelphia: J. B. Lippincott.

Weaver, S. M., Broome, A. K. & Kat, B. J. B. (1978). Some patterns of disturbed behaviour in a closed ward environment. *Journal of Advanced Nursing, 3*, 251-263.

Wells, D. A. (1972). The use of seclusion on a university hospital psychiatric floor. *Archives of General Psychiatry, 26*, 410-413.

Werner, P. D., Rose, T. L., Yesavage, J. A. & Seeman, K. (1984). Psychiatrists' judgments of dangerousness in patients on an acute care unit. *American Journal of Psychiatry, 141*, 263-266.

Werner, P. D., Yesavage, J. A., Becker, J. M. T., Brunsting, D. W. & Isaacs, J. S. (1983). Hostile words and assaultive behavior on an acute inpatient psychiatric unit. *Journal of Nervous and Mental Disease, 171*, 385-387.

West, D. A., Litwok, E., Oberlander, K. & Martin, D. A. (1980). Emergency psychiatric home visiting: Report of four years experience. *Journal of Clinical Psychiatry, 41* (4), 113-118.

Westermeyer, J. & Kroll, J. (1978). Violence and mental illness in a peasant society: Characteristics of violent behaviors and "folk" use of restraints. *British Journal of Psychiatry, 133*, 529-541.

Wexler, D. B. (1982). Seclusion and restraint: Lessons from law, psychiatry, and psychology. *International Journal of Law and Psychiatry, 5*, 285-294.

Wexler, D. B. (1984). Legal aspects of seclusion and restraint. In K. Tardiff (Ed.), *Psychiatric uses of seclusion and restraint* (pp. 111-124). Washington, DC: American Psychiatric Press.

Whaley, M. S. & Ramirez, L. F. (1980). The use of seclusion rooms and physical restraints in the treatment of psychiatric patients. *Journal of Psychiatric Nursing and Mental Health Services, 18* (1), 13-16.

Whitehead, J. A. (1975). Violence in institutions. *International Journal of Offender Therapy and Comparative Criminology, 19*, 87-89.

Whitman, J. (1979). When a patient attacks: Strategies for self-protection when violence looms. *RN, 42* (9), 30-33, 114.

Whitman, R. M., Armao, B. B. & Dent, O. B. (1976). Assault on the therapist. *American Journal of Psychiatry, 133*, 426-429.

Wiggins, J. S. (1973). *Personality and prediction: Principles of personality assessment.* Reading, MA: Addison-Wesley.

Wood, K. A. & Khuri, R. (1984). Violence: The emergency room patient. In J. T. Turner (Ed.), *Violence in the medical care setting: A survival guide* (pp. 57-83). Rockville, MD: Aspen.

Woody, R. H. & Associates. (1984). *The law and the practice of human services.* San Francisco, CA: Jossey-Bass.

Yamaguchi, N. G. (1972). *The fundamentals of Goju-Ryu karate.* Burbank, CA: Ohara.

Yamaguchi, N. G. (1974). *Goju-Ryu karate II.* Burbank, CA: Ohara.

Yesavage, J. A. (1983a). Bipolar illness: Correlates of dangerous inpatient behaviour. *British Journal of Psychiatry, 143*, 554-557.

Yesavage, J. A. (1983b). Inpatient violence and the schizophrenic patient. *Acta Psychiatrica Scandinavica, 67*, 353-357.

Yesavage, J. A. (1984). Correlates of dangerous behavior by schizophrenics in hospital. *Journal of Psychiatric Research, 18* (3), 225-231.

Yesavage, J. A., Werner, P. D., Becker, J., Holman, C. & Mills, M. (1981). Inpatient evaluation of aggression in psychiatric patients. *Journal of Nervous and Mental Disease, 169*, 299-302.

Zavodnick, S. (1984). Psychopharmacology. In W. R. Dubin, N. Hanke & H. W. Nickens (Eds.), *Psychiatric emergencies* (pp. 55-75). New York: Churchill Livingstone.

Zitrin, A., Hardesty, A. S., Burdock, E. I. & Drossman, A. K. (1976). Crime and violence among mental patients. *American Journal of Psychiatry, 133*, 142-149.

Zold, A. C. & Schilt, S. N. (1984). Violence: The child and adolescent patient. In J. T. Turner (Ed.), *Violence in the medical care setting: A survival guide* (pp. 85-105). Rockville, MD: Aspen.

Zunin, L. M. & Barr, N. I. (1971). How to handle psychiatric emergencies in a general hospital. *Resident and Staff Physician, 14* (4), 61-65.

AUTHOR INDEX

SUBJECT INDEX*

* Italic indicates illustration; "t" following page number indicates table.

criteria for, 20, 87-89
disagreement concerning,
    88-89
environmental safety, 118
firearm defense, 118
hostage situations, 119-120
judgment and, 74-75, 121
manual restraint, 121, 131-143,
    133-143
    precautions for, 131-134
    rationale for, 121, 131-132
mechanical restraint, 131-147
    devices, 145-147
    precautions for, 144-145
    rationale for, 143-144
necessity of, 17-19
principles of, 74-84, 75t, *78, 80,*
    81, 83, 84-86, *85*
psychological orientation for,
    74-75, 85
striking and grabbing defenses,
    90-118, *91, 93, 95-98, 99-104,*
    106-110, 112-113, 116-117
Precautions, 50, 64, 66, 124-125
Prevention
    physical intervention in, 86, 90,
        92, 111, 113, 123
    primary, 19, 22
    secondary, 22
    tertiary, 23
    therapeutic milieu and, 86
Psychological aspects of aggres-
    sive behavior
    anger, 29, 33, 50-53
    communication, 30-33
    context, 28-29
    fear, 29, 33, 50-53
    natural controls, 29-30
Purposiveness of behavior, 26

Relationship, therapeutic, 42-43

Seclusion
    precautions for, 126
    procedures, 127-131
    rationale for, 125-126
    room characteristics, 126-127
    training effects upon use of, 19
Situation
    aggressive behavior and, 28-29
    clinical technique and, 42

Teamwork
    incident review, 125
    interclinician communication,
        123-124
    violence precautions, 124-125
Training
    content of, 155-156
    cost-effectiveness of, 155
    disagreements concerning,
        88-89
    effects of, 19-21, 154
    implementation of, 156-158
    instructional techniques,
        159-164
    instructor qualifications,
        157-158
    legal necessity of, 19-21,
        154-155
    liability release for, 167,
        178-179
    objectives of, 154, 155, 176
    opposition to, 19-20, 153-154
    physical exercises, 167-174
    psychological exercises,
        164-166
    purpose of, 20
    requirements for, 153
    safe practice rules, 167-168
    sample program, 175
    social norms and, 154
    "standard of care", 63, 154